# DOES FAMILY PRESERVATION SERVE A CHILD'S BEST INTERESTS?

*Controversies in Public Policy*
edited by Rita J. Simon


**Howard Altstein** *personally dedicates this book to his granddaughters, Audrey Altstein Bachman and Lois Altstein Bachman.*

**Ruth McRoy** *personally dedicates this book to her grandsons, Nicholas Desmond Constable and Jordan Christopher Shearer.*

❏

*This book is also generally dedicated to the thousands of children in the child welfare system— may they find permanence.*

# DOES FAMILY PRESERVATION SERVE A CHILD'S BEST INTERESTS?

Howard Altstein and
Ruth McRoy

GEORGETOWN UNIVERSITY PRESS / WASHINGTON, D.C.

Georgetown University Press, Washington, D.C.
© 2000 by Georgetown University Press. All rights reserved.
Printed in the United States of America.

10 9 8 7 6 5 4 3 2 1                              2000

This volume is printed on acid-free offset book paper.


**Library of Congress Cataloging-in-Publication Data**

Altstein, Howard.
    Does family preservation serve a child's best interests? /
Howard Altstein, Ruth McRoy.
        p. cm.— (Controversies in public policy)
    Includes bibliographical references and index.
    ISBN 0-87840-786-3 (cloth : acid-free paper)—
ISBN 0-87840-787-1 (paper :acid-free paper)
    1. Child welfare. 2. Kinship care. 3. Adoption. 4. Family.
I. McRoy, Ruth G. II. Title. III. Series

HV713 .A544 2000
362.7—dc21                              00-026363

# Contents

# List of Tables

# Authors' Biographies

**Howard Altstein** earned his B.A. from Brooklyn College in 1959 and his Master's in Social Work from New York University in 1962. He has worked as a social worker in juvenile justice, foster care, and in school systems. After receiving his Ph.D. from the University of Illinois, Urbana, in 1971, he was a Lecturer at the Hebrew University School of Social Work. He is a professor at the University of Maryland School of Social Work where he has taught since 1972. In 1992 and 1993 he was a consultant to the Romanian Committee on Adoption in Bucharest. In 1995 he was awarded a Fulbright to the Department of Social Work, Ben-Gurion University in Beersheva, Israel. Professor Altstein is the coauthor of several books on transracial and intercountry adoption.

**Ruth G. McRoy** received her B.A. in Psychology and Sociology and her Master's in Social Work from the University of Kansas, Lawrence. She received her Ph.D. in Social Work from the University of Texas at Austin in 1981. Prior to joining the University of Texas faculty in 1981, she was on the faculty at the University of Kansas, Lawrence, and at Prairie View A&M University in Prairie View, Texas. Dr. McRoy holds the Ruby Lee Piester Centennial Professorship in Services to Children and Families and is the Director of the Center for Social Work Research at the School of Social Work at the University of Texas, Austin. She holds a joint appointment at the U.T. Center for African and African American Studies. She is the coauthor of several books and many articles on adoption.

# Preface

In this seventh volume in the Pro and Con Series on Public Issues, two distinguished professors of social work assume opposing positions on which policies are most likely to serve the best interests of children. Ruth McRoy argues that children should remain with their biological parents until and unless they, the parents, have demonstrated that they are hopelessly incapable of providing their children with a stable, loving home. For their own protection, the children might have to be temporarily removed from their parents' home until the mother (for example) has overcome her drug addiction, and the father has undergone therapy for his violent behavior, and drinking or other abusive behaviors have been controlled. During this period, which could last for several years, the child, Professor McRoy and other family preservationists argue, should not be placed in foster care or made available for adoption. The best choice is to place the child in the care of a relative. The homes of grandparents or aunts and uncles are the most likely and desirable placements. The child then has not been cut off from his/her blood relatives and the desired return to the parents' home is made easy and relatively smooth. Not only are the child's interests acknowledged, but the family has also been preserved. Ruth McRoy argues and provides data to support her position that family preservation should be the ultimate goal in satisfying both the child's and the parents' best interests.

Professor Howard Altstein strongly disagrees. His review of empirical studies provides two basic results. First, that families whose behavior originally necessitated removal of their children are not likely to undergo sufficient change as to allow them to provide a healthy environment for their children. They are simply dysfunctional, and treatment, even imprisonment, is not likely to bring about the desired changes in the behavior and attitudes of the mother or father, or both. Or, if changes do occur, they will take years; and the children during this period are left in limbo. At best, they are temporary guests in their relatives' homes, and at worst, they are moved back and forth from their parents' homes to institutions. Why not, Altstein argues, free these children for adoption as soon as possible and give them a chance to live secure and stable lives with families who want, and are prepared, to love them. The research Altstein cites indicates highly successful adjustment rates for children who have been adopted. And, Altstein emphasizes, it is the children and their best interests that should be the focus of our attention and around which policies should be determined.

There you have it. Should the emphasis be placed on preserving the biological family, the children as well as the parents, or should the major concern focus on the children and freeing them for adoption as soon as possible? One, two, or more years in a child's life can determine his or her entire future. Which author's position do you find most persuasive?

Rita J. Simon
School of Public Affairs
American University
1999

# PART ONE

# Ruth McRoy
*Family Preservation's Essential Services in the New Millennium*

CHAPTER ONE

# Introduction

The merits of family preservation programs have been debated for many years; recent media accounts of child fatalities in families that receive family preservation services (Ingrassia and McCormick 1994) have fueled the controversy even further. Unfortunately, the debate has revolved around an all-or-nothing philosophy about the disposition of child abuse and neglect cases: provide family preservation services, or place the child in out-of-home care and then terminate parental rights and place the child for adoption. In reality, arguments supporting either option are simplistic, as neither solution can be viewed as the only option for all children who have suffered abuse or neglect in their families of origin.

Family preservation is based on the philosophy that persons can best develop if they are able to remain in their own family or rely on their family as a resource. Thus, the family, community, family members' culture, ethnicity, and religious background are all viewed as strengths which can be used as helping resources (Ronnau and Marlow 1993).

As I will show, family preservation can work successfully and is needed by many families and children. In cases in which children cannot remain with their birth parents, efforts should be made to place them with extended kin before considering adoption by nonrelatives. This monograph will address each of these options and identify systemic as well as familial factors associated with the removal of children from birth families and placement in out-of-home care. Since African American children are overrepresented among children in the nation's foster care system, particular attention will be given to outcomes for this population.

The rest of this chapter examines the philosophical, historical, and legislative bases for the development of family preservation programs. Chapter 2 provides an overview of theories guiding the practice. Evidence of effectiveness of family preservation and the significance of kinship care as a form of family preservation are discussed in chapter 3. The fourth chapter delineates policies and practices that have historically affected and are currently influencing adoption outcomes, especially for African American children, and the final chapter offers recommendations for the continuation of family preservation services in the new millennium.

## ☐ HISTORICAL BACKGROUND

Our society has always grappled with the competing values that children should be protected from abusive and neglectful parents, yet children have a right to be raised by their biological parents. A historical look at the disposition of child abuse cases reveals not only that family preservation is not a new idea, but that the practice and policy emphasis on child removal and family preservation has varied over time.

### Early Child Saving

The English Poor Law of 1601 established the doctrine of *parens patriae*, which justified governmental intervention in the parent-child relationship in cases in which parents were not fulfilling their responsibilities as parents or cases in which substitute care was needed. Typically, these were cases in which children came from impoverished families or children were "orphaned, abandoned, or unsupervised" (Schene 1998, 25). In the 1700s and 1800s, dependent children were often sent either to foundling hospitals or placed in almshouses alongside adults who were poor and/or sick. Older children were often indentured to families or placed in apprenticeship positions to learn a trade. The public took responsibility for the care of children of the "unworthy poor," but service delivery was generally provided under private auspices. Children's institutions were later established as a result of the problems associated with children and adults being placed together in almshouses.

In the nineteenth century, Charity Organization Societies and other charitable organizations advocated for rescuing and protecting children from abusive or neglectful environments, impoverished situations, and "inadequate parents" through family foster care. There were many cases of child vagrancy among poor and immigrant parents who were unable to provide for the needs of their children. Typically, if this came to the attention of authorities, the child was removed from the parents and placed in a foster home or institution or sent far away to a farm in the Midwest. Minuchin (1974, cited in Nelson 1997) referred to this as "parentectomy."

A pioneer in the "child-saving" movement, Charles Loring Brace established the Children's Aid Society in 1853 in order to provide for the needs of the growing number of unattended children in large urban areas. Over a 75-year period, this agency sent over 150,000 homeless children by train to live with Midwestern Christian farm families (Schene 1998). Brace's "child-saving" remedy was based on his belief that children would benefit by being placed in the homes of farmers, whom he believed to be "our most solid and intelligent class" (Brace 1872, 225).

Some criticized Brace's philosophy as prejudicial against immigrants, and many expressed concern that (1) Catholic and Jewish immigrant children were being placed mostly with Protestant families, and (2) the foster families were not properly investigated or supervised. Nevertheless, many children continued to be removed and placed in "foster homes" and the debate continued as to whether foster homes or institutions were better arrangements for dependent children (Costin 1985).

Great attention was also given during this time to the need to intervene and rescue children who were being treated cruelly by parents. Organizations to prevent cruelty to animals had been in existence for some time, but nothing comparable was in place for children. Initiated in part by attention to the case of "Mary Ellen," a little girl who had been beaten and left alone for hours, the New York Society for the Prevention of Cruelty to Children was formed in 1877, and the first law protecting children from abuse was passed in New York. Gradually, Societies for the Prevention of Cruelty to Children were established in many more cities and additional state laws were passed to protect children (Schene 1998).

## Early Family Preservation

By the late 1800s and early 1900s, efforts were under way to try to preserve families rather than always removing children from impoverished biological families. Early social work pioneers Mary Richmond and Jane Addams argued that children should not be removed from their families due to poverty, and efforts should be made to preserve families (Bremner 1972; Warsh, Pine, and Maluccio 1995). Through the early settlement houses, attempts were made to improve the quality of urban life, reform child labor, and enhance community stability (Berry 1997).

In 1909, the White House Conference on the Care of Dependent Children took the following position on the removal of children: ". . . Except in unusual circumstances, the home should not be broken up for reasons of poverty, but only for considerations of inefficiency or immorality" (Bremner 1971, 365). Thus, a differentiation was made between families of worthy character and the unworthy, undeserving poor.

However, by 1933, there were 243,000 children living in out-of-home care (5.8 children per 1,000 children in the child population). Many of these children were from poor families. In 1935, the Social Security Act was passed to provide a financial safety net for families to keep them from falling into poverty. This law defined child welfare services as public social services to protect and care for homeless, dependent, and neglected children as well as children in danger of becoming delinquent (Samantrai 1992). Through the Aid to Dependent Children program, established by the Social Security Act, cash assistance was provided to poor single mothers to care for their children in their homes. Although Title IV-B of the Social Security Act provided grants to states to fund preventive and protective services, states still used funds primarily for out-of-home foster or institutional placements for children (Schene 1998).

In 1959, Maas and Engler and others expressed grave concern about "foster care drift," that is, the growing number of children growing up in foster care and often moving from one family to another. Although foster care was to be a "temporary service," it was clear that children were languishing in the system, moving from one place to another, and minority children were disproportionately represented in care (Maas and Engler 1959; Shyne and Schroeder 1978). Most of the children in care had been removed from poor families, and many were experiencing developmental delays, low self-esteem, and other emotional problems stemming from their experiences of separation and loss (Pecora et al. 1992b). However, in the 1960s, despite these growing concerns about the effects on children growing up in the system, children continued to be removed from abusive families, partly due to research reports suggesting that abuse and neglect stemmed from inter-generational pathological problems. Therefore, child removal was seen as the best solution.

Over the years, the competing interests of child removal versus family preservation have flourished. Federal and state legislative mandates requiring reporting of abuse and neglect cases and availability of funds to support out-of-home placements have led to increased child removals and placements in foster care. For example, beginning in 1961 the federal government made open-ended funds available for out-of-home placement when Title IV-A of the Social Security Act was modified to include Aid to Families with Dependent Children (AFDC) payments for individual states' foster care programs. In that year alone, 150,000 children were placed in out-of-home care. The Child Abuse Prevention and Treatment Act (CAPTA) of 1974 and the Child Abuse Act Amendments of 1984 called for mandated reporting of suspected child maltreatment. This legislation provided grants to states for child abuse investigations as well as prevention and treatment programs and community-based family resource centers (Courtney 1998). The increased reporting led to more investigations and child removals.

Although Title XX of the Social Security Act allocated additional funds to states for child abuse and neglect services, by the late 1970s, 75 percent of the funds were still being used for foster care instead of family support and preservation (Burt and Pittman 1985). By 1977, 500,000 children were living away from their families in foster care (Shyne and Schroeder 1978) and the average length of time in care was 2.4 years. This represented not only an increase in the number of children in care, but an increase in the length of time in care (MacDonald 1994).

The majority of the children being removed from their families histori-cally and currently have been from low-income backgrounds, and many are ethnic minorities. In the late 1970s, these groups began to challenge such out-of-home placement practices. For example, American Indian children had been routinely removed from their tribes and reservations and placed in boarding schools or with white foster or adoptive families. Opposition to this practice led to the Indian Child Welfare Act of 1978 (PL 95-608), which specified priority for kinship care or placement of Indian children in extended families; if those were not possible, placement in Indian foster families was the preferred alternative. Although the Act was designed to facilitate placement and preservation of Indian families and culture, funding for services was insufficient (Pecora et al. 1992b). As with the American Indian population, other populations of color and child advocates expressed a growing concern about the large number of minority children who seemingly were removed from their families because their parents were poor or minorities (Ingrassia and McCormick 1994) and remained in the foster care system indefinitely.[1]

## Permanency Planning Initiative

In response to the growing numbers of children in care, federal policy on child welfare services was redefined through Public Law 96-272 (Saman-trai 1992) in 1980 as part of the Adoption Assistance and Child Welfare Act.

Basically, the law stipulated that the government would assume responsibility to help families so that they would not fail in child rearing, instead of punishing families for failure. This "permanency planning" legislation was designed to expedite decision making to facilitate children either being maintained in their own homes or placed quickly into permanence in adoption. Funds were provided for adoption assistance for families adopting special needs children (Courtney 1998).

Although child welfare services were originally designed to protect and promote the welfare of children, and to prevent or remedy problems that might result in neglect or abuse, PL 96-272 also stipulated that child welfare services should prevent the unnecessary separation of children from their families, and called for the restoration of children to families from which they had been removed. According to the law "in each case, reasonable efforts will be made (a) prior to the placement of a child in foster care, to prevent or eliminate the need for removal of the child from his home, and (b) to make it possible for the child to return to his home" (PL 96-272). The law further stipulated that failure to comply could result in loss of federal funds for foster care and adoption assistance. Case plans were required for each case, including a justification of the foster care placement, a description of the services offered and the services provided to prevent removal of the child from the home and to reunify the family.

Public Law 96-272 stipulated that the order of permanency planning outcomes should be as follows: reunification with the child's family, adoption, guardianship, and long-term foster care (Barth and Berry 1987). Moreover, the law was designed to ensure that children were placed in the least restrictive (most family-like) environment and preferably close to the home of the family of origin. At that time, if reunification could not be achieved within 24 months, adoption was considered the next preferable option.

The implementation of this law temporarily reduced the numbers of children in out-of-home care (Hartman 1993). By 1985, approximately 286,000 children were in foster care (Newlin 1997), about 220,000 fewer children than in 1977. However, after President Carter left office, the Reagan administration attempted unsuccessfully to repeal PL 96-272. Nevertheless, new regulations were issued that did not specify minimum standards; programs and implementation were left up to individual states. The program was never adequately funded (Samantrai 1992). Ironically, an analysis of the impact of PL 96-272 on states' child welfare services in 1985–1986 revealed that prevention efforts were lower in states that had higher proportions of children living below the poverty level (Newlin 1997).

In the late 1980s, however, foster care placements started to rise again as more infants and children of drug-addicted parents were removed from their birth families due to abuse and neglect. The growing incidence of AIDS, teen parenthood, poverty, and violence also influenced the increase in children coming into care. Between 1976 and 1993, child abuse and neglect reports increased by more than 347 percent (Schene 1998). In 1995, 3.2 million children were reported as alleged victims of maltreatment (Courtney 1998).

According to statistics provided by the American Public Welfare Association, in 1992 approximately 429,000 children were in foster care (McKenzie 1993), a 53-percent increase from 1987 (see Table 1). Of this number, only about 15 to 20 percent of these children had adoption plans (McKenzie 1993). By 1994, there were an estimated 462,000 children living outside of their homes (MacDonald 1994), and in 1995, the number had risen to an estimated 486,000 (Child Welfare League of America 1998).

Estimates in 1997 suggested that about 500,000 children were in care (Zumwalt 1997), and approximately 100,000 would not be returning to their biological families. Interestingly, Barth (1997) observed that this increase was due in large part to the low rate of discharging children from care, rather than the increase in foster care entrants.

Another factor, often de-emphasized, which may contribute to the fluctuation in numbers of children in foster care, is the funding stream. Reimbursements to states for foster care payments and adoption assistance programs is open-ended and dependent on the number of children placed in out-of-home care and the cost of their care. Unlike foster care, prevention, family preservation, and other child welfare services have fixed funding streams. Therefore, fiscal incentives exist for public agencies to place children in out-of-home care rather than provide services to prevent placements (Courtney 1998, 92).

A recent report from the General Accounting Office (U.S. House 1997) reveals that the federal government supports the maintenance of a large out-of-home placement system. In 1995, states received more than $2.8 billion in federal assistance for about half of the estimated 494,000 children in care. These costs are expected to rise to $4.8 billion by 2001, as the number of children in care will increase by almost 26 percent. Total annual expenditures for foster care nationwide is between $10 billion and $12 billion (U.S. House 1997). Although funding for foster care has increased, and the number of reports of child abuse and neglect has risen astronomically over the past few years, funding for investigations and family support services has not risen accordingly (Courtney 1998).

**TABLE 1.** Comparison of Children in Care by Year

| Year | Number of children in foster care | Rate of children in care per thousand children under 18 years |
|------|-----------------------------------|----------------------------------------------------------------|
| 1933 | 243,000 | 5.8 |
| 1961 | 244,500 | 3.7 |
| 1977 | 503,000 | 7.6 |
| 1987 | 300,000 | 4.8 |
| 1994 | 462,000 | 6.8 |

Source: Adapted from Pelton, L. 1997. Child welfare policy and practice: The myth of family preservation. *American Journal of Orthopsychiatry* 67:546.

## ❑ RENEWED INTEREST IN FAMILY PRESERVATION

Concomitant to the increase in the number of children in care, there has been a decrease in the number of foster families available to provide temporary care for these children. For example, in 1984, there were approximately 147,000 foster parents, but by 1990, the number had dropped to 100,000 (National Commission on Foster Family Care 1991). The decline has been due in part to the growing economic necessity of dual-earner households, the geographic mobility of families, concerns about behavioral problems of children in care, growth in single-parent households, and increase in divorce rates, as well as the increasing cost of child rearing (Berrick 1998).

Partly in response to the decline in the number of foster families, the growing number of children in care, and limited funding for family preservation and support, in 1993, as part of the Omnibus Budget Reconciliation Act (PL 103-66), the federal government established the Family Preservation and Support Services Program (FPSSP). Almost $1 billion was distributed to states over a five-year period (Ahsan 1996). States were encouraged to use the new funding along with other funding sources to "integrate preventive services into treatment-oriented child welfare systems and to improve service coordination" (158). States were required to establish an integrated continuum of services for families at risk or in crisis, including reunification or permanency planning, preplacement/preventive services, follow-up services, respite care, and parent skills training (Newlin 1997).

Actually, before the federal mandate, a number of states had already instituted family preservation programs as part of their continuum of treatment services. By 1991, 12 states had programs mandated by statute and 31 states had such policies as part of their legislative agenda (Smith 1993).

Despite the $1 billion funding for family preservation services, the federal budget for foster care over the same five-year period will probably exceed $16 billion. Thus, the two types of services are in no way equal in terms of funding (Courtney 1998).

## Facilitating Adoptions and Preserving Birth Families

The plight of children in foster care again came to the nation's attention in 1996, when President Clinton announced a plan to double the number of children being placed in adoption or in permanent legal guardianships by the year 2002 (Child Welfare League of America 1997). In order to accomplish this goal, Congress passed the Adoption and Safe Families Act of 1997 (PL 105-89), which calls for the Department of Health and Human Services to set annual adoption targets for each state, with states receiving per-child bonuses for placements made beyond their annual targets. The federal government will give cash bonuses of $4,000 for each child adopted exceeding the previous year's number, and an additional $2,000 for each adoption of a child who is older or has some physical or emotional disability. Moreover, this federal legislation requires states to set up a permanent placement plan for a child after one year in care, instead of 18 months under prior rules.

PL 105-89 also reauthorized family support and family preservation services and increased their funding level by about $20 million a year. The name of the program was changed to "Promoting Safe and Stable Families" in order to emphasize the outcome of safety and stability rather than a particular type of service delivery program. These changes came about partly due to criticisms of family preservation programs. According to the Adoption and Safe Families Act of 1997 (PL 105-89), "reasonable efforts" toward family preservation and reunification efforts are not required if a parent has:

. . . subjected the child to "aggravated circumstances" such as torture, abandonment, or chronic abuse; Murdered or been responsible for the unlawful death of another of his or her children; Committed a felony assault that resulted in serious bodily injury to the child or another of the parent's children; or Had his or her parental rights involuntarily terminated before.

If reasonable efforts are not required, then a state has 30 days to hold a permanency planning hearing for the affected child. If reasonable efforts have been made to reunite, permanency hearings must be held within 12 months after the child is considered to have entered care.

This law also calls for concurrent planning to "identify, recruit, process, and approve a qualified family for an adoption" while filing a termination of parental rights petition, in order for workers to simultaneously plan for more than one possible outcome (Kroll 1998). Although family-centered approaches are noted in the new law, they are considered as part of a continuum of services designed to protect children, support families, and promote permanency and adoption (McCroskey and Meezan 1998).

## Poverty and Child Maltreatment

Child maltreatment is no longer viewed as solely the result of parental psychopathology, necessitating child removals. Recent research has demonstrated that child maltreatment is a result of multiple risk factors outweighing protective factors. According to Wells and Tracy (1996, 673),

> these risk factors include child factors such as handicapping condition; parent factors such as aggressive personality; marital factors such as domestic violence; family factors such as presence of a chaotic family system, social isolation, and unemployment; neighborhood factors such as a geographic area containing a concentration of impoverished people; and cultural factors such as norms promoting the use of violence.

Moreover, the child's age and developmental stage also play an important role in assessing risk and protective factors. Increased poverty and substance abuse have been identified as factors influencing the growth of maltreatment (Wells and Tracy 1996). Although poverty does not cause maltreatment, "the effects of poverty appear to interact with other risk factors such as unrealistic expectations, depression, isolation, substance abuse, and domestic violence to increase the likelihood of maltreatment" (English 1998, 47).

The Third National Incidence Study of Child Abuse (1996) reported that "the incidence of abuse and neglect is approximately 22 times higher among families with incomes less than $15,000 per year than among families with incomes of more than $30,000 per year" (Courtney 1998, 95). It is also important to note that physicians and other service providers may be more likely to attribute an injury to abuse in cases of children in lower-income homes and attribute the same injury to an accident in higher-income families (Newberger et al. 1977; O'Toole, Turbett, and Nalpeka 1983). These differential attributions and labeling bias against low-income families may account for some of the relationship found between poverty and abuse.

## ❏ CONCLUSIONS

The debate over family preservation is not new. Our society has continually grappled with the concept of *parens patriae*, as well as policies to address the problem of dependent poor children. As the number of children in poverty has grown, along with a rise in reports of child abuse and neglect, the foster care system is now overloaded as it strives to accommodate the large numbers of children coming into care. It is clearly not a perfect system, with children remaining in care for an average of two years and often being moved several times while in care. Minority children are disproportionately represented among children in poverty and among children in out-of-home care.

Although the emphasis of social policy legislation has vacillated over time among child removal, family preservation, and adoption, funding streams have primarily emphasized removal of children and placement in care. Because about a half million children are currently in care out of their homes, we must again examine the options that are realistically available for them and their families. The next chapter provides an overview of family preservation services and the theories on which this practice is based.

## ENDNOTE

**1.** Adoption agencies had been established in the early part of the century primarily under private nonprofit agency auspices and served mostly white childless couples. Since black children were excluded from these segregated adoption services (Billingsley and Giovannoni 1972; Day 1979) as well as from many institutions, they were typically placed in foster care. If it were not for the extensive informal adoption network that has existed in the black community since the time of slavery, even more black children would have entered and remained in the foster care system.

CHAPTER TWO

# Overview of Family Preservation

Part of the controversy over family preservation comes from a misunderstanding of the concept. According to Hartman (1993, 511), "The term 'family preservation' has become so popular that anybody doing anything helpful in relation to a family could claim they were doing it. Multiple definitions make the term meaningless."

Some define family preservation as a practice or program model (Kinney, Haapala, and Booth 1991), others as a philosophy guided by values and principles (Ronnau and Sallee 1993), a service delivery model (Henggler, Melton, and Smith 1992), and as a policy (Adoption Assistance and Child Welfare Act of 1980; Omnibus Budget Reconciliation Act of 1993; Wells and Tracy 1996). Warsh, Pine, and Maluccio (1995, 625) call for a broad definition and suggest that it is

> . . . a philosophy that supports policies, programs and practices that recognize the central importance of the biological family to human beings. It underscores the value of individualized assessment and service delivery, with adequate system supports, in order to maximize each family's potential to stay together, or again become safely connected.

When defined as a practice model, it is often used interchangeably with Homebuilders, a short-term intensive intervention model. As a philosophy, the concept represents a continuum of services that may include family reunification and placement prevention, but may also include foster care, residential care, termination of parental rights, or open adoption, all of which include contact with the family of origin (Warsh, Pine, and Maluccio 1995). The family preservation philosophy is based on the following assumptions:

- It is the parents' right to raise their children if at all possible. Most abusive parents do not intend to harm their children (Berliner 1993).
- Child abuse stems from a variety of causes, not just parental psychopathology as originally thought. External stressors such as poverty, racism, and social isolation, in addition to factors such as substance abuse, depression, developmentally inappropriate expectations of children, or child temperament might also be associated with child abuse.
- Children flourish in situations of continuity and stability, and we should do whatever is necessary to keep the child safe. However, if at all possible, the parent-child bond should be maintained and unnecessary state intervention avoided (Goldstein, Freud, and Solnit 1973).
- Biological connectedness is very important to a child's identity and separations between parent and child can be devastating (Whittaker and Tracy 1990). Children who are removed from their birth families suffer a loss that can be quite traumatic. According to Fahlberg (1991), children separated from their parents may have responses that range from severe depression to almost no reaction. In the former case, these children may have been very attached to a parent or parents, and in the latter case, the child may have been emotionally neglected or abused and may feel no connection to the family of origin. Generally, the strength of the relationship and abruptness of the loss will influence how one deals with separation from parental figures (Fahlberg 1991).
- After children have been removed from a chaotic, conflictual, and abusive family situation, many have a negative self-image, feeling responsible for the removal or deserving of rejection. Once placed in care, if the child experiences additional separations through multiple placements, his/her sense of lovability, security, and stability will be further undermined. Feelings of loss may trigger rage and a sense of helplessness and powerlessness (Steinhauer 1991).
- Families have strengths and the capacity for growth and change (McCroskey and Meezan 1998). An empowerment model approach helps clients identify their needs and empowers them to be resourceful in solving their problems. Not only are the problems that come to the

attention of the system (i.e., abuse and neglect) addressed, but also issues which the family identifies, such as lack of transportation, and so forth (Hagedorn 1995).

- Appropriate supports and interventions may resolve the problem and enable the parents to effectively care for their children (Berliner 1993).

Family preservation and family support are often discussed as parts of a continuum of family-centered services designed to overcome threats to family stability. Although federal legislation (Omnibus Budget Reconciliation Act of 1993, PL 103-66) uses the terms "family support" and "family preservation services," it is important to note the distinction between these types of services. Family support services are designed to prevent problems from arising in child rearing and are provided before a crisis occurs. Family preservation services are mandatory and are designed for families whose children are at risk for removal or for families in which children have been removed, but have a goal of reunification. These intensive family preservation services are provided in the home (Savage 1998).

Family preservation services are generally characterized as being brief and concentrated and most often delivered directly by children's protective services or by private agencies that contract with the state. They can be delivered in order to bring about a behavior change in the family, create a safe environment for the child, and prevent removal. In addition, such services may be called for once a child has been removed as a result of child maltreatment. In these cases, family preservation is used when the goal is to return the child to the family. Services may be provided by a team of people including case managers, foster parents, foster care workers, and others as needed (Savage 1998). Concrete services such as transportation are provided as well as family counseling. Usually delivered in the family's home, family preservation typically includes all family members in the intervention (McCroskey and Meezan 1998).

## ❏ THEORETICAL BASES OF FAMILY PRESERVATION

Family preservation as an intervention model draws heavily from several theories including crisis intervention, family systems, social learning, and the ecological perspective (Barth 1990). Recently, two other theories, attachment and functional (Grigsby 1993), have also been noted to contribute significantly to the principles of family preservation services. All six theories will be discussed in this section.

*Crisis Intervention Theory.* Family preservation services are crisis-oriented, the crisis being the imminent removal of the child. According to the theory, a crisis occurs when a hazardous event has not been resolved through customary responses, leading to disequilibrium and emotional upset (Caplan 1964). At this time of disequilibrium, the individual or family feels so vulnerable that they are willing to try new behaviors in an attempt to regain equilibrium (Barth 1990). However, this "window" for introducing new and hopefully more adaptive coping behaviors is time limited; the family is thought to regain a form of equilibrium within four to six weeks. Thus, the brevity of family preservation services stems from the assumption that changes are most easily implemented during this short time frame (Golan 1984).

*Family Systems Theory.* The family systems approach to family preservation maintains that the family develops structures to carry out its functions, and these structures can be functional or dysfunctional depending on the specific family tasks and the family context (Barth 1990). Any particular family member's behavior problems are believed to be a reflection of other problems within the family. Treatment focuses on the family as a whole and is designed to assist family members in meeting their needs in functional and satisfying ways (Nelson, Landsman, and Deutelbaum 1990). Structural family therapy views families as dynamic systems in which the structure of the family determines the effectiveness of its functioning. Family structures are examined in terms of boundaries, alignments, and power (Minuchin 1974). Programs based on a family systems approach base their therapy on these constructs, preferring to see all family members simultaneously in order to identify maladaptive systemic relationships (Berry 1994). Family preservation often works to establish the parental subsystem as possessive of authority and to delineate family boundaries (Whittaker, Kinney, et al. 1990).

*Social Learning Theory.* This theory (Bandura 1977) examines cognition and expectations, and the ways in which they influence behavior and change. Family preservation programs that utilize social learning theory as their foundation stress the importance of behaviors and interactions within the family that cause risk of placement. Social learning theory asserts that rewards and punishments influence the likelihood that certain parent and child behaviors are repeated and that this likelihood is mediated by expectations. Modeling is an important means of transmitting effective ways of interacting and is often employed by home-based therapists. Other interventions derived from social learning theory include parent training, parent consultation, communication and problem solving training, role playing, and behavior modification (Barth 1990), as well as techniques such as family therapy, crisis intervention, casework, homemaker services, and advocacy (Hinckley and Ellis 1985). The Homebuilders model of family preservation relies heavily on these techniques (Whittaker, Kinney, et al. 1990).

*Ecological Theory.* This perspective is crucial to family preservation as it emphasizes the environmental influences on the family and emphasizes that individuals cannot be understood apart from their interactions with their environments (Berry 1994; Barth 1990). Problems are viewed as a mismatch between the capabilities of the family and the demands of the environment. Parents and children are treated as partners with caseworkers in the process of strengthening the family. The main goal of ecologically based programs is to assess the resource deficits of families and to link them with available resources in their extended family, neighborhood, and community so as to enhance the functioning of their social network (Tracy and McDonell 1991). As such, the environment is used as both the source of and solution to problems. Intervention is primarily carried out in the home and includes any services the family needs to stay intact (Berry 1992).

*Attachment Theory.* According to this theory (Bowlby 1969 and 1980; Ainsworth 1985), early relationships between child and caretaker influence the child's subsequent relationships. Child welfare service providers must also consider attachments to siblings and grandparents. The threat or actual loss of a relationship may lead to anxiety, grief, and sorrow. According to Grigsby (1993, 21),

> the decision to remove a child from the family in order to "protect" the child must be weighed against the possibility of traumatizing the child in the process of out-of-home placement. The trauma of separation from parents, grandparents, siblings may generate feelings of helplessness, anger and fear.

However, if the child has experienced life-threatening injuries from caretakers, the child should be placed in another environment so that the child may have the opportunity to develop positive attachment relationships and experience continuity of relationships, essential to the child's healthy development (Goldstein, Freud, and Solnit 1973, 31, cited in Grigsby 1993).

*Functional Theory.* A traditional social work theory, the functional perspective emphasizes the essential nature of client empowerment and growth, and views the client as a partner in the change process (Taft 1937; Smalley 1967; University of Pennsylvania School of Social Work 1990). The worker is involved in contributing to planned change by linking clients to needed resources as well as seeking changes in the social service system. It calls for time-limited services in which the structure and function of the agency provide the context for intervention. This is consistent with the family preservation approach as these workers help clients utilize their own strengths, focus on present-day realities, and offer very time-limited specific structured services designed to prevent out-of-home placement (Grigsby 1993).

## ❏ MODELS OF FAMILY PRESERVATION SERVICES

Typically, family preservation services can be divided into two categories: rehabilitative and intensive. Rehabilitative family preservation services are less intensive and are used in cases in which future removal of a child is possible. Services are provided such as parent education, anger management, behavioral techniques, and assertiveness training, in addition to concrete services such as transportation, emergency financial assistance, and help with housing or clothing.

When placement of a child is imminent or in cases in which family reunification is planned, intensive family preservation services are offered. These programs are similar to rehabilitative ones, but are time limited, and provide intensive help on immediate problems. Caseloads consist of two to six families at a time; workers spend four to twenty hours each week with a family and are on call at all times. Usually lasting between four and twelve weeks, families are typically seen in their homes (McCroskey and Meezan 1998). Despite what some believe (Ingrassia and McCormick 1994), family preservation does not mean leaving a child in danger. When a child is at imminent risk of harm, family preservation calls for removal of the child (Hagedorn 1995).

Nelson, Landsman, and Deutelbaum (1990) developed a typology consisting of three models of family-centered services whose goals are tertiary prevention, prevention of out-of-home placement, or reunification of children with families from which they have been removed. The three models are described below.

*Crisis Intervention Model.* This model is based on the belief that intervention within 24 hours of referral, low caseloads, service delivery in the home, provision of concrete and supportive services, and on-call therapists who design interventions that fit each family's needs will help families avoid placement of their children. Homebuilders—often used synonymously with this model—was developed in Tacoma, Washington, in 1974, long before the term "family preservation services" was created during the early 1980s. It has been modeled by many other programs and is often used as a prototype of a family preservation program (Forsythe 1992). A brief history of the development of this program is provided below.

David Haapala and Jill Kinney, psychologists who worked with emotionally disturbed children in residential treatment, applied for funding to the National Institute of Mental Health (NIMH) to develop a "super" foster home to help foster parents care for emotionally disturbed adolescents. NIMH challenged them to develop a program to keep the original birth family intact. As a result, this couple developed Homebuilders, a program to help Tacoma families in their own homes instead of resorting to out-of-home care. In the early 1980s, the Edna McConnell Clark Foundation began funding programs designed to reduce the unnecessary placement of children in out-of-home care. After funding 12 different programs over six years, they discovered that one of the programs, Homebuilders, was especially effective for many children as it reduced placements (Forsythe 1992).

The Homebuilders model calls for short-term (six weeks to three months), home-based intensive intervention based on crisis theory (MacDonald 1994). Typically, workers have three to six cases, meet clients in their homes, and may be on call 24 hours a day. Services include concrete services for the entire family such as transportation, as well as client empowerment and skill building (Pecora et al. 1990).

Supporters of PL 96-272 (Adoption Assistance and Child Welfare Act) developed pilot programs to prevent placement and some modeled their own after Homebuilders. By 1992, almost 30 states had Homebuilder-type programs.

Although the original program in Tacoma was designed to address family conflicts involving primarily angry, oppositional white adolescents, it has also been used in urban areas, where the population consisted of primarily minority families that were characterized by substance abuse and intergenerational poverty. Families often consisted of single parents, children, extended family members, and sometimes stepparents and/or boyfriends who may have periodically resided in the home.

Critics of family preservation have suggested that the original Homebuilders model was developed for two-parent or stable one-parent families and cannot be successfully applied to dysfunctional families (MacDonald 1994). However, according to statistics on Homebuilders, the program prevented placement over 90 percent of the time and a year's follow-up revealed an 80-percent avoidance rate. The safety record of this program is almost 100 percent (Forsythe 1992).

*Home-Based Model.* Although in many ways similar to the crisis intervention model, the home-based model incorporates longer-term interventions and is based on family systems theory. FAMILIES, a prototypical home-based program, began in West Branch, Iowa, and was designed to prevent out-of-home placement of adolescents. Some describe the methods utilized in the home-based model as "pretherapeutic." Therapists see the family in the home, carry a caseload of ten to twelve, and see families an average of 4.5 months (Nelson, Landsman, and Deutelbaum 1990, 9). Studies of placement prevention rates using this model have revealed about 80 percent placement prevention rates. Project Kaleidoscope in Chicago, Illinois, is the model standard.

*Family Treatment Model.* Based on family systems theory, this model emphasizes treatment of the entire family; however, direct provision of concrete services is less likely. Typically, workers carry caseloads of 11, have a 90-day treatment period, and intervention may involve co-therapists. It is less intensive and can be implemented in an office or home setting. This approach was first utilized through the state of Oregon's Children's Services Division. Studies have revealed that 90 percent of families remained together after 90 days and 66 percent had had no placements and were together at the end of 12 months.

The selection of the most appropriate program model may vary by age of child, type of family problem, and need for short- or longer-term assistance. Home-based programs serve the fewest families, but are geared toward low-income, single-parent families with young children at risk for abuse and neglect and who may need longer-term service. Crisis intervention and family treatment programs can serve more families and tend to benefit families that need brief assistance (Nelson, Landsman, and Deutelbaum 1990).

## ☐ CONCLUSIONS

Family preservation programs have increased dramatically since 1982, when only 20 programs were in existence. By 1988, there were 333 programs located in more than 25 states (Ronnau and Marlow 1993). Family preservation services can be offered at a substantial savings compared to traditional foster care or residential programs. As family foster care can cost at times as much as $10,000 per child per year, and hospitalization as much as $100,000 per year, family preservation is a bargain at a rate of between $3,000 and $5,000 per child per year (Forsythe 1992).

Although some critics suggest that attempts to preserve families have led to child deaths, a careful review of the child death statistics reveals that about one-tenth of one percent of abuse and neglect cases result in a child death and many of these cases were never reported to Child Protective Services (CPS). In Michigan's Families First family preservation program, out of 40,000 children served, there have been two fatalities, occurring during the first two years of this ten-year-old program (Nelson 1997). Family preservation, like any other program, is clearly not the panacea in all cases, but it has been effective in many. Outcome evaluation studies of family preservation services and kinship care are addressed in the following chapter.

CHAPTER THREE

# Empirical Support for Family Preservation and Kinship Care

*With Cinda L. Christian and Elizabeth E. Thompson*

All home-based programs share certain basic characteristics in that they "all are committed to maintaining children in their own homes whenever possible, to focusing on entire families rather than individuals, and to providing comprehensive services that meet the range of families' therapeutic, supportive, and concrete needs" (Nelson, Landsman, and Deutelbaum 1990, 4). Despite these common goals, each family preservation program draws upon a particular theoretical framework, which in turn influences the type and means of intervention. As mentioned in the previous chapter, although both functional and attachment theories form much of the conceptual framework for family preservation, the three main theories in the literature guiding home-based family preservation models are social learning theory, family systems theory, and ecological theory. To date, most evaluations of such programs use prevention of placement as the only index of program success; few programs assess whether family members have indeed gained skills that persist in their relations with family after intervention, and none have compared outcomes for children who have been placed for adoption versus receiving family preservation services while remaining in their own biological family homes.

The following discussion reviews the research regarding family preservation programs to determine the extent to which research supports the three theories behind the models and supports the clinical effectiveness of the model, indexed by prevention of out-of-home placement. Another form of family preservation that has been found to be successful for many families, kinship care, is also discussed in this chapter.

# ❏ SOCIAL LEARNING PRACTICE MODELS

Family preservation programs that utilize social learning theory as their foundation stress the importance of behaviors and interactions within the family that can increase the risk of placement. The main focus of these programs is improving dyadic interaction patterns in the family rather than requiring the simultaneous participation of all family members (Berry 1994). Social learning theory asserts that rewards and punishments influence the likelihood that certain parent and child behaviors are repeated and that this likelihood is mediated by expectations. Modeling is an important means of transmitting effective ways of interacting and one that is employed by home-based therapists. Social learning models attempt to identify patterns of family interaction that are detrimental to competent family membership. Interventions derived from social learning theory include parent training, parent consultation, communication and problem solving training, and behavior modification (Barth 1990), as well as techniques such as family therapy, crisis intervention, casework, homemaker services, and advocacy (Hinckley and Ellis 1985).

Research regarding the general concepts of social learning theory demonstrates that rewards, penalties, and expectations are developed both through direct experience and observation (Barth 1990). While social learning-based interventions have proven successful with families presenting a range of difficulties, including child conduct disorders, marital discord, and juvenile delinquency (Gurman, Kniskern, and Pinsof 1986), one author has reported a "lack of direct evidence about the effectiveness of [this] approach in addressing families that are neglecting, abusing, or sexually mistreating their children" (Barth 1990, 100).

However, there is increasing evidence of clinical success of social learning-based methods. A number of research studies have been focused on Homebuilders, the first and most prevalent family preservation program. Homebuilders combines a social learning-based emphasis on expectations, behavior modification, and skill development, with an approach gleaned from crisis intervention theory that views families as most open to change during a period of crisis. The proliferation of Homebuilders programs has resulted in a proliferation of studies evaluating their success (see Table 2). As with most studies of family preservation and home-based programs, social learning-based programs judge "success" as the proportion of families avoiding the placement of their child or children outside the home. A survey of the programs presented in Table 2 shows the generally high rates of success defined in this fashion for these various programs. In a study that examined the use of a social learning-based program with multiproblem families, Szykula and Fleischman (1985) found that a control group had a higher prevention rate (55%) than the treatment group (36%), although this difference was not significant. This finding suggests that this method may work well with less disturbed families but may need to be modified to counteract the many problems present in some families.

Some studies have evaluated outcomes of social learning interventions by examining factors other than simply prevention of placement. Treatment families have demonstrated substantial reductions in physical and verbal violence (Hinckley and Ellis 1985), as well as improvements in children's school adjustment, delinquent behavior, home-related behavior, and in parents' supervision of young children, parenting of older children, attitudes toward preventing placement, and knowledge of child care (Pecora, Fraser, and Haapala 1987, cited in Berry 1994). Smith (1995) noted improvements in marital and family communication patterns, intrafamily relationships, home maintenance, use of community resources, and child-rearing behavior as a result of worker modeling and teaching in a family preservation program. Clients rate the programs highly; one study reported that 63 percent of successful families and 66 percent of families with out-of-home placements rated the program as either extremely or moderately helpful, with placement and non-placement groups agreeing on which critical events of the therapy were most helpful (Fraser and Haapala 1987). This latter finding suggests that global self-reports of helpfulness are not predictive of placement outcome. A second evaluation of a Homebuilders program (Behavioral Sciences Institute 1987) reported very similar satisfaction rates after 12 months: 63 percent said the intervention was very helpful, and 18 percent found it to be helpful. Fraser and Haapala (1987) also reported that the provision of concrete assistance resulted in more successful outcomes, a finding that supports the emphasis on such assistance that is the cornerstone of intensive family-based programs.

As mentioned in the preceding chapter, after 16 years, Homebuilders has a record of preventing placement over 90 percent of the time. Even after one year of completing the program, the placement avoidance rate is above 80 percent (Forsythe 1992).

Rodenhiser, Chandy, and Ahmed (1995) published the findings from year one of a ten-year longitudinal study of intensive family preservation services using the Homebuilders model. This is one of few studies that have

**TABLE 2.** Comparison of Social Learning Family Preservation Programs: Proportion of Families Avoiding Placement

| Program | Sample size | Length of treatment | Success at termination | Success after 3 months | Success after 12 months | Success of control group |
|---|---|---|---|---|---|---|
| Homebuilders, Washington (Kinney, Madsen, Fleming, and Haapala 1977)[a] | 80 | 1.5 months | 90% | | 97% (of previous 90%) | |
| (Fraser and Haapala 1987) | 41 | 2–5 months | | 52% | | |
| (Behavioral Sciences Institute 1987)[b] | 444 | 1 month | | | 87% | |
| (Pecora, Fraser, Haapala, and Bartlomé 1987)[b] | 216 | 1 month | 82% | | | |
| (Haapala and Kinney 1988) | 678 | 1 month | | | 87% | |
| (Kinney, Haapala, Booth, and Leavitt 1988)[a] | NR | NR | 73%*  80% | | | 28%  0% |
| (Stroul 1988)[a] | NR | NR | 92% | | | |
| Homebuilders, New Jersey (Feldman 1990) | 96 | 1.5 months | | | 54% | 42% |
| (Pecora, Fraser, and Haapala 1992) | 453 | NR | | | 93% | |

| Program | Sample size | Length of treatment | Success at termination | Success after 3 months | Success after 12 months | Success of control group |
|---|---|---|---|---|---|---|
| Homebuilders, Florida (Paschal and Schwahn 1986)[a] | NR | NR | 95% | | 84% | |
| Homebuilders, Maine (Hinckley 1984)[b] | NR | 2 months | 82% | | | |
| (Hinckley and Ellis 1985) | 134** 25 | 2 months | 76% 90% | 84% NR | | |
| Homebuilders, Oregon (Szykula and Fleischman 1985)[a] | NR | NR | 92%*** 36% | | | 62% 55% |
| Utah Family Preservation (Callister, Mitchell, and Tolley 1986)[a] | 168 | 3 months | 85% | | | |
| (Pecora, Fraser, Haapala, and Bartlomé 1987)[b] | 120 | 2 months | 71% | | | |

NR = Not reported.

*First number is for group with status offenses; second number is for group with mental health issues.

**Two separate programs were examined.

***First number is for families without serious problems; second number is for multiproblem families.

[a]Cited in Nelson, Landsman, and Deutelbaum (1990).

[b]Cited in Berry (1994).

27

used standardized measures to assess family risk and child well-being. They reported significant changes in parent-centered risk and parental disposition and in child-centered risk and child performance after the intervention. However, no differences were found in economic risk and household adequacy, such as food, clothing, housing, utilities, and money management.

## ❏ FAMILY SYSTEMS PRACTICE MODELS

As mentioned in chapter 2, the family systems approach to family preservation maintains that the "general structures that a family develops to carry out its functions can be functional or dysfunctional depending on the specific family tasks and the family context" (Barth 1990). Any particular family member's behavior problems are believed to be reflecting other problems within the family. Treatment focuses on the family as a whole and is designed to assist family members in meeting their needs in functional and satisfying ways (Nelson, Landsman, and Deutelbaum 1990). Programs based on a family systems approach prefer to see all family members simultaneously in order to identify maladaptive systemic relationships (Berry 1994).

The studies that have been conducted demonstrate the utility of this type of home-based intervention. The rates of placement prevention presented in Table 3, ranging from 55 to 88 percent, are impressive and point to the effectiveness of this method.

Schuerman, Rzepnicki, and Littell (1992a) reported the findings of their study of the Illinois Family First Initiative through the Department of Children and Family Services. This study, referred to as the most rigorous large-scale evaluation yet conducted on a family preservation program (Courtney 1997b; Epstein 1997), included almost 1,600 families (995 in Family First and 569 in regular services). The program was implemented through contracts with private agencies. The median length of service was 108 days, although 40 percent were served for more than 120 days. The authors reported that 77 percent of the families in the program remained intact and 81 percent of the children avoided placement one year after referral (Epstein 1997).

One study (AuClaire and Schwartz 1986) found no difference between the treatment and control groups in the number of placement episodes even though the treatment group was 55 percent successful in avoiding placement. These results suggest that this treatment may not prevent placements but can increase the likelihood of the children being returned home.

**TABLE 3.** Comparison of Family Systems Family Preservation Programs: Proportion of Families Avoiding Placement

| Program | Sample size | Length of treatment | Success at termination | Success after 3 months | Success after 12 months | Success of control group |
|---|---|---|---|---|---|---|
| FAMILIES, Iowa (Bryce 1978)[a] | NR | 4.5 months | 85% | | | |
| Family Studies Project Hennepin County, Minnesota (AuClaire and Schwartz 1986)[b] | 55 | 1 month | 55% | | | * |
| Maryland Intensive Family Services (Pearson and King 1987)[a] | 80 | NR | 83% | | | (N=180) 67% |
| Oregon Intensive Family Services (Showell 1985)[b] | 261 | 3–4 months | 88% | | | |
| Oregon High Impact (Allen 1985)[b] | NR | 3–4 months | | | 87% | |
| Ramsey County, Minnesota (Lyle and Nelson 1983)[b] | 34 | 1 month | 76% | | | 55% |
| Family Program, Virginia (Bribitzer and Verdieck 1988) | 42 | NR | 73% | | | |
| Families First, Illinois (Schuerman, Rzepnicki, and Littell 1994) | 995 | 3–4 months | | | 81% | (N=569) |

NR = Not reported.

*There was no difference between the treatment group and a control group in the number of placement episodes; no information on percentage of control group families avoiding placement was provided.

[a]Cited in Nelson, Landsman, and Deutelbaum (1990).

[b]Cited in Berry (1994).

Families participating in family systems-based programs who were successful in avoiding placement evidence other benefits of the intervention. Some of these benefits include improvements in behavior, material resources, family dynamics, emotional climate, employment, housing, community involvement, protection of the child from the abuser, and support for the primary caregiver (Berry 1991; Nelson, Landsman, and Deutelbaum 1990). Even families who experienced an out-of-home placement exhibited improved behavior, emotional climate, family dynamics, and community involvement (Berry 1991).

## ◻ ECOLOGICAL PRACTICE MODELS

Ecological models are particularly concerned with environmental influences on the family and emphasize that individuals cannot be understood apart from their interactions with their environments (Berry 1994; Barth 1990). Parents and children are treated as partners with the caseworkers in the process of strengthening the family, and the goals the family identifies as being important are emphasized rather than a goal chosen by the caseworker to modify family structure (Berry 1991). The main goal of ecologically based programs is to assess the resource deficits of families and to link them with available resources in their extended family, neighborhood, and community so as to enhance the functioning of their social network (Tracy and McDonell 1991). As such, the environment is used as both the target of and resource for change. Intervention is primarily carried out in the home and includes any services the family needs to stay intact (Berry 1992).

The ecological model particularly relies on resources outside the family to affect and maintain change. An analysis of the resources drawn upon by clients served by the Emergency Family Care Program reports that while only 11 percent of the clients contacted friends, 10 percent contacted their church, and 10 percent contacted family members, clients did utilize a wide range of community agencies and resources (Berry 1994). These results suggest that the ecological model is correct in attributing an important influence to community resources but may be overly optimistic in predicting the utilization of family and friends to provide for needs such as transportation, child care, and so forth.

Data on the clinical effectiveness of ecologically based family intervention programs is provided in Table 4. Rates of prevention of placement ranging from 97 percent at termination to 75 percent after 12 months are very high and supportive of the ecological approach. However, when outcomes other than placement are examined, a less optimistic picture emerges. Of the 367 families followed in the Emergency Family Care Program, Berry (1994) reports that one-fifth of them declined in successful use of child discipline and general child care. Families that made gains in household cleanliness and physical condition of the building were success-ful in avoiding placement. Berry (1994) also found that families with a mentally incapacitated caregiver or a history of child neglect may be the least likely to benefit from these specific services.

## ☐ CHALLENGING CRITICS OF FAMILY PRESERVATION

Despite the apparent success of many family preservation interven-tions, opponents of family preservation generally identify weaknesses of the research, such as the lack of comparison or control groups, short-term follow-up data only or the complete lack of follow-up data, small samples, reliability and measurement validity problems, the use of placement avoid-ance as the sole outcome criteria, or failure to distinguish between families who are reunified and those never separated (e.g., Wald, Carlsmith, and Leiderman 1988; Barth 1990; McDonald and Marks 1991; Wells and Biegel 1991; Rossi 1992, Thieman, and Dail 1992; and Berry 1994). Although I acknowledge there is a need for more controlled and better qualitative assessments of outcomes, the data on avoidance of placement suggest that these interventions are working in the short term and that we need to extend the period of service and assess what types of services may be most effective over time with particular families. Moreover, it is also important to acknowledge that there may be cases in which temporary placement is a positive outcome to enable a family to work on specific issues; these child and family successes should also be measured. At times, placements are made due to an administrative judicial decision that may not be directly related to case characteristics (Rossi 1992, 92).

More qualitative investigations are needed, including process evalu-ations on program development, perceptions of family preservation work-ers, and families' perceptions of treatment (Wells and Biegel 1992). Drake et al. (1995) have conducted one of the very few investigations of consumer and provider views on family preservation. They noted that lack of acces-sible information on service availability, lack of emergency funds for a family's immediate needs, lack of affordable housing and adequate shelters to accommodate homeless families, lack of transportation, and disrespectful treatment by workers were all barriers to service effectiveness.

The outcome research that is often used to criticize family preservation programs often includes studies of older children with behavioral problems,

**TABLE 4.** Comparison of Ecologically Based Family Preservation Programs: Proportion of Families Avoiding Placement

| Program | Sample size | Length of treatment | Success at termination | Success after 3 months | Success after 12 months | Success of control group |
|---|---|---|---|---|---|---|
| Emergency Family Care, Alameda County, California (Berry 1994; 1992; 1991) | 40 | 3 months | 90% | 85% | 75% | |
| Emergency Family Care, San Francisco, California (Berry 1994; 1992; 1991) | 327 | 3 months | 97% | 93% | 90% | |
| Intensive Family Services, Nebraska (Leeds 1984)[a] | 21 | 5 months | 86% | | | |

[a]Cited in Berry (1994).

while others look only at children who are much younger and abused or neglected (Bath and Haapala 1994). Type of problem, age of child, and drug involvement all may be factors that will affect outcome. The types of services received and characteristics of the child and family must also be factored into an evaluation of results. In many of the evaluations, it is unclear what services were being received by controls and whether the experimental treatment was sufficiently different from services received by the control group (Rossi 1992).

## ☐ BENEFITS OF FAMILY PRESERVATION SERVICES

All three of the above theoretical approaches have been shown to be successful when success is defined as avoidance of out-of-home placement. Social learning-based and family systems-based approaches have both proven successful with the family-centered approach (Barth 1990; Nelson, Landsman, and Deutelbaum 1990). Limited research has been conducted on ecologically based programs, but the research presented here suggests the effectiveness of this approach for avoidance of placement. It has been argued that programs drawing mainly from social learning theory provide greater assistance through the use of more behavior-changing strategies (Barth 1990), but the emphasis on the provision of concrete services underlying all family preservation programs seems to ensure their success. Given the success of these approaches individually, a synthesis of these three approaches may be warranted, as the "core helping skills that are common to family systems and social learning approaches may make a difference to families—especially if they are buttressed by the timely provision of work in the family's broader ecology" (Barth 1990, 107).

In addition, another aspect of family preservation services that supports its continued use is its low cost relative to out-of-home placement. For example, Forsythe (1992) estimates that family foster care can cost an average of $10,000 a year, while family preservation costs from $3,000 to $5,000 per family (for four to six weeks of intervention). This low cost, combined with the short-term nature of the intervention, makes family preservation programs a desirable option to child protective agencies.

We need to explore what types of family preservation services work for what types of clients and the relative effectiveness of different approaches to placement prevention (Schuerman, Rzepnicki, and Littell 1994). Clearly, many programs are successful, but we need a better understanding of how and for whom a particular intervention works.

The finding that children who remain in their homes sometimes have less desirable outcomes than children placed in foster care, when factors other than avoidance of placement are taken into account, suggests that more funding needs to be put into prevention so that families can be supported and preserved before they are at risk for out-of-home placement (Barth and Berry 1987). Rather than looking at avoidance of placement as a successful outcome, researchers also must look at the overall outcome for the child. Barth and Berry (1987, 86) noted,

> If lifetime relationships are the goal of permanency planning (and family preservation)—as we believe they should be—then the length and level of support available for special-needs adoption, guardianships, long-term foster care, and, especially, family reunification are glaringly shortsighted.

Future research should attempt to determine the most effective elements of service, the clients best suited for family preservation services, and the best method for delivering these services. Moreover, legislative entities are needed that mandate greater funding and support for family preservation services.

The following section introduces kinship care, another form of family preservation that involves removing the child from her/his birth parents and placing him or her with relatives. This approach preserves biological connectedness and maintains continuity in family relationships for children.

## ❑ KINSHIP CARE AS A FORM OF FAMILY PRESERVATION

Kinship care is defined by the Child Welfare League of America (1994) as "the full-time parenting and protection of children by relatives, members of their tribes or clans, godparents, stepparents, or any adult to whom a child, child's parents, and family members ascribe a family relationship." Because kinship care "enables children to live with people they know and trust, supports the transmission of children's family identity, supports the child's ethnic and cultural identity, helps children stay connected to brothers and sisters, and helps children retain or build connections to the extended family members," it is considered by many agencies to be another strategy for family preservation (Scannapieco and Hegar 1996, 568).

The practice of extended kin taking care of children in cases of dependency or hardship is not new. In many cultures, including those of Africa and the Pacific Islands, and especially in the African American,

Hispanic, and Native American cultures, children have been cared for by kin (Hill 1977; Trattner 1994; Hegar and Scannapieco 1999). However, kinship care has only recently been utilized as a formal child placement alternative. This shift toward kinship care began with the passage of the Indian Child Welfare Act of 1978, which formally established a hierarchy of preferred placements (relatives, members of the tribe, members of other Native American groups, non-Native Americans). The practice of kinship care solidified in 1979 when the Supreme Court ruled that kin must be given equal opportunity to qualify for foster parent status (*Miller v Youakim* 1979). The concept of kinship placement was then acknowledged as a placement option with both a cultural and legal basis. Currently, kinship care is the fastest growing type of out-of-home placement in the United States (Gleeson 1996). The *New York Times* (Daley 1989) reported that "in less than three years, the number of children in [kinship care in New York] has grown to 19,000 more children than were in the city's entire foster care system two years ago" (cited in Walker, Zangrillo, and Smith 1994). By 1990, more than half of the total foster care population in New York City was placed with relatives (Walker, Zangrillo, and Smith 1994), and relative placements in Illinois and California were later reported to exceed 59 percent and 40 percent, respectively (Gleeson 1996).

In recent years, when a child in the United States needs to be moved out of her/his home due to abuse or neglect, many state and private agencies' first response is to find an appropriate relative who is willing to care for the child. In part, this is likely to be due to the recent decrease in the number of traditional foster homes available, coupled with the increase in children needing placement. According to the National Foster Parents Association, in 1992 there were about 100,000 foster parents and about 442,000 foster children (Ryan 1995). In addition, as mentioned in chapter 2, the Adoption Assistance and Child Welfare Act of 1980 (PL-96-272) mandate that children be kept in the least restrictive environment possible is reflected in the shift in child welfare philosophy and practice toward family preservation. Although the care of children by relatives is a common practice throughout the world, the placement of children with relatives is a fairly new practice for child welfare agencies (Simpson 1994). Kinship care is consistent with the notion that children are best served in their own families and is a form of family preservation. Preliminary findings suggest that children in kinship foster care tend to do slightly better than those in family (nonrelative) foster care on certain outcome measures, and experience more stable placements (e.g., Dubowitz and Sawyer 1994b; Iglehart 1994; LeProhn and Pecora 1994).

## Characteristics of Kinship Care Providers

Although there is no national picture of what kinship care families look like, there have been several studies that focus on specific agencies or geographic areas. Probably the closest approximation of a national sample of kinship families was gathered by LeProhn and Pecora (1994) in a study of the Casey Family Program foster parents. The Casey Family Program is a privately funded foster care agency that primarily enlists children who are in need of long-term care and is noted for exceptional commitment to the children it serves. Adults who were Casey foster children often credit the agency for their success and ability to break the cycle of abuse in their biological families (Fanshel, Finch, and Grundy 1989). As of August 1994, 30 percent of the Casey children were formally placed with relative foster caregivers. Surveys were mailed to all foster parents in the 13 states that the agency serves, with a response rate of 76 percent (284 surveys returned). This study found that a large portion of kinship caregivers were single parents (54.9%); in contrast, nonrelative caregivers were almost twice as likely as kinship families to be headed by married couples (80% versus 45%, respectively). Most of the kinship caregivers were grandmothers (54%) or aunts (38%), with a significant proportion of these families being financially stressed in caring for these children (34% had an annual income of less than $10,000, including the foster care maintenance payments, compared to only 2% of nonrelative caregivers). There was also a significant overrepresentation of minority families who were kinship foster families: while the overall sample consisted of 53% white, 21% African American, 12% Native American, and 11% Latino families, 70% of kinship care was provided by minority families compared to only 28% of traditional foster care. In addition, the data indicated that while there was no statistically significant difference in the amount of time the kinship versus nonrelative foster children spent in care (despite a slightly longer period for kinship children), the kinship children had significantly more stable placement histories, with an average of 3.24 placements versus 6.3 placements for nonrelative foster children.

LeProhn and Pecora (1994) found that kinship foster parents saw themselves more in the role of sharing responsibility with the agency to help the children maintain contact with birth family members. Possibly as a partial result of kinship foster parent perceptions, the kinship care children often did better than their nonrelative foster counterparts at maintaining contact with their birth family members.

Other studies of more geographically limited samples have found kinship family profiles to be similar to those found by LeProhn and Pecora

(1994). For example, studies of kinship care in the cities of Baltimore, Berkeley, Los Angeles, and Philadelphia, and the states of Illinois, Michigan, and New York all reveal that the majority (most well over 80%) of kinship care children in these regions are also African American (Benedict, Zuravin, and Stallings 1996; Berrick, Barth, and Needell 1994; Dubowitz, Feigelman, and Zuravin 1993; Iglehart 1994; Ingram 1996; Link 1996; Mayor's Commission for the Foster Care of Children 1993; Mills and Usher 1996; Testa et al. 1996; Thornton 1991). Many also specify that the child is most likely to be living with a grandmother (Dubowitz, Feigelman, and Zuravin 1993; Link 1996; Mayor's Commission for the Foster Care of Children 1993) or other relative, most likely a woman (Ingram 1996) who is significantly older than the average family foster care provider (Berrick, Barth, and Needell 1994; Mayor's Commission for the Foster Care of Children 1993). More than half of the kinship caregivers in many of the studies have annual incomes significantly less than foster parents (e.g., Berrick, Barth, and Needell 1994), with some studies finding a majority of kinship foster parents making less than $10,000 per year (Dubowitz, Feigelman, and Zuravin 1993; Mayor's Commission for the Foster Care of Children 1993), and one (Thornton 1991) finding that 45 percent of kinship caregivers have incomes below $5,000 per year. Several also found that less than half of the kinship caregivers had completed high school (Berrick, Barth, and Needell 1994; Dubowitz, Feigelman, and Zuravin 1993; Testa et al. 1996; Thornton 1991). Dubowitz, Feigelman, and Zuravin (1993) and Berrick, Barth, and Needell (1994) also mirrored LeProhn and Pecora's (1994) finding that there were more single caregivers raising the kinship children than the foster children (51.7 to 53% versus 24.1%, respectively). The reported income differential is likely to be related to other differences between kinship and traditional foster care, such as the greater likelihood that a kinship caregiver is less educated and a single, female head of household. However, greater placement stability was experienced by kinship children than other foster children (Dubowitz, Feigelman, and Zuravin 1993; Iglehart 1994), which is supported by additional findings that the majority (68% and 60%, respectively) of children in kinship care were in their original placement home (Mills and Usher 1996; Testa et al. 1996).

Regardless of all the similarities of findings in different geographic areas, there are still some discrepancies. While Dubowitz, Feigelman, and Zuravin (1993) found that kinship children were placed in care for the first time at a younger age, LeProhn and Pecora (1994) and Iglehart (1994) found no significant age differences between the kinship and foster children. In addition, several studies found different, although related, reasons why kinship children entered out-of-home care. Children were placed with relatives most commonly due to neglectful parental care (Dubowitz, Feigelman, and Zuravin 1993; Iglehart 1994; Mills and Usher 1996), neglectful care coupled with parental drug addiction (Gleeson, O'Donnell, and Bonecutter 1997), or parental drug exposure or substance abuse (Link 1996; Task Force on Permanency Planning for Foster Children 1990), which presumably were associated with neglectful care.

## State and Agency Policy and Practice

*Recent Trends.* Simpson (1994) surveyed 59 Child Welfare League of America member agencies regarding their kinship care practices and policies. One of the most revealing findings from the 30 survey responses received was that a vast majority of agencies, public agencies in particular, do not keep records on kinship care families. This does not mean that they had no information about the placements, but, generally, kinship care families were not separated from the rest of their foster care families or child protective services cases. Many agencies were unable to provide such basic information as the estimated number of families in their agency that would be classified as kinship care families, and some were even unwilling to guess as to the demographics of these families. Although the agencies' inability to provide basic information was important in itself, other important contributions to the knowledge about agency practice were provided by this study. The findings that 90 percent of agencies reported an increase in the number of kinship care arrangements over the past five years and 89 percent reported that kinship care was now the first option explored when the parent-child relationship was disrupted were particularly significant. In addition, half of the agencies reported that while they consider kinship care a form of out-of-home placement, they philosophically view kinship care as family support and family preservation.

A few researchers have been fortunate to have samples that included both kinship care children and traditional foster care children. For instance, Berrick, Barth, and Needell (1994) used a sample of 246 children in kinship care and 354 children in foster care drawn from the University of California at Berkeley Foster Care Data Base. Despite the difference in ethnic composition between kinship care and traditional foster care children (kinship: 43% African American, 34% white, 17% Hispanic; foster: 21.8% African American, 62.8% white, 9.1% Hispanic) similar to differences reported in family profile studies (e.g., LeProhn and Pecora 1994), children across these two groups remained similar in several important ways. Both kinship and foster children were judged to be in good or excellent health by their caregivers. Although both groups were having more problems than children not in placement, they did not differ from each other on measures of behavior or school activities. However, the kinship children did have fewer structural school problems than children in foster care (i.e., kinship children were less likely to have repeated a grade or to be enrolled in special education classes). This study implies that kinship children are not disadvantaged by their placement with a relative caregiver and may actually be slightly advantaged when compared to foster children on some outcomes.

In a large sample of adolescents in Los Angeles County placed out of their homes (352 in kinship care, 638 in nonrelative foster care), Iglehart (1994) found that there were no significant differences between kinship and foster children in the areas of educational performance and behavior problems in school. Unfortunately, both groups in this study were doing equally poorly, with over one-third of each group performing below grade level, and nearly one-third of each group having behavior problems serious enough to be noted in case files. However, significant differences were discovered in the area of mental health functioning; 18 percent of foster children versus only 10 percent of children in kinship care were reported to have serious mental health problems. Iglehart concludes that the data do not support "any of the extant suppositions about the noxious effects of kinship care on children or their adjustment" (119). In contrast to the alluded-to suppositions, data from this study also support the observation that kinship foster children are as well off, if not better, than their traditional family foster care counterparts.

However, similar to other studies (e.g., Berrick, Barth, and Needell 1994; Dubowitz, Feigelman, and Zuravin 1993; and Lewis and Fraser 1987), Iglehart (1994) found that kinship care children did not receive the same level of monitoring by the caseworker as did the (non-kin) foster children (2.1 versus 3.3 visits in a six-month period).

# ❑ CONCLUSIONS

Kinship care is increasingly being used as a family resource, especially for large numbers of African American children. Most of these children are living with a grandmother or other female relative. These kin placements have been found to be typically more stable than foster placements. As more and more children come to the attention of the child welfare system due to drug use by parents and parental neglect of children, public agencies are finding that kin are able to provide for their needs and in many states, kinship care is the first option explored when children have to be removed from their birth families. Since kinship providers clearly need more resources than traditional foster parents, much more attention must be given to providing supportive as well as economic services to better meet their needs and improve outcomes for children.

Despite the merits of family preservation and kinship care, some believe that children who have been abused or neglected by their birth families should have an opportunity to be adopted by the hundreds of thousands of people who are seeking to be parents. These proponents feel that efforts should be made to reduce the number of children lingering in foster care by expediting the termination of parental rights of birth parents and making their children available for adoption. Moreover, they believe that an option for the disproportionately high number of African American children in the foster care system is transracial placement with white adoptive families. Chapter 4 examines factors that influence the growing number of children—particularly African American children—in foster care, and explores the option of adoption for these children.

# CHAPTER FOUR

# Adoption Challenges

Before considering the viability of adoption as an option for children needing permanence, it is important to understand the types of children who are in the nation's foster care system. As mentioned in chapter 2, according to the National Adoption Information Clearinghouse (NAIC, 1998), in 1996 there were approximately 500,000 children in foster care. Of this number about 4% are less than a year old, 29% are between ages 1 and 5; 27% are between 6 and 10; 25% are between 11 and 15; and 14% are between 16 and 18. Thus, the majority, 67%, are age 6 and older. About 51% are male and 49% female. For 54%, the majority, the case plan goal is family reunification. Besides the 16% who have adoption as their case plan, the remainder will have as their goal to live with relatives, long-term foster care, emancipation, or guardianship. Almost 70% of the children in care have been there for at least one year. Sixty-five to 85% of children entering the foster care system have at least one sibling and 75% of sibling groups are separated from one another after they enter foster care (NAIC 1998).

Minority children are more likely to be overrepresented in the foster care system. Forty-five percent are African American, 14% Hispanic, 1% Asian/Pacific Islander, and 2% American Indian. Thirty-eight percent are white. In some urban areas, 80% to 90% of the children in care are children of color (McRoy 1994). Morton (1993, 1) commented:

> Overrepresentation in foster care is a polite way of saying that our child protection system more frequently separates African American children from their birth families, and keeps them separated, than it does White children.

Studies have documented that children of color do remain in care longer and receive fewer services than white children and that their families have fewer contacts with workers than white families (Close 1983; McRoy 1996). According to the National Black Child Development Institute (1989), black children enter care around age seven and spend an average of two years in care. It is likely that they will have at least two caseworkers, change schools, and move at least two times. Thus, these children will have experienced losses and transitions, and often experience placements with families of a different cultural background from what they are accustomed to (McDonald & Associates 1992; McRoy 1996).

The welfare reform law (PL 104-193, Personal Responsibility and Work Opportunity Reconciliation Act) passed in 1996 that established Temporary Assistance to Needy Families (TANF) might also have implications for the increase of all children, yet disproportionately minority children, in out-of-home care. The law calls for five-year time limits on assistance as well as the possible loss of entitlement in cases of drug-related crimes or substance abuse. This law may affect approximately 3 million children as benefits are reduced or cut off entirely for low-income families. Many families may find that low-wage jobs will not provide sufficient income to adequately raise their children and children may be at greater risk for neglect or abandonment (Courtney 1998). As funds for child welfare services other than out-of-home care are limited, it is likely that the number of foster care entrants will significantly increase.

In addition, because many families may lose entitlement to services due to substance abuse problems or drug-related crimes, over 2.5 million children may be affected. Moreover, research suggests that a combination of lack of sufficient economic resources and parental difficulty in performing the parental role increases family stress. Some predict that the reduction of the economic and health supports in AFDC food stamps and Medicaid will lead to more family problems in low-income families. Others disagree and suggest that families will become better functioning once they have greater economic self-sufficiency and parents receive employment and parent training as part of the welfare reform bill (Thieman and Dail 1997).

In the event the former prediction is accurate, funding is available for more out-of-home care if needed. PL 104-193, like previous legislation, protects the funding of out-of-home care under Title IV-E. "Although meeting pre-1996 AFDC eligibility requirements will no longer insure a child's eligibility for welfare assistance in a parent's home, it will continue to qualify the child for federal foster care assistance in someone else's home" (Allen 1996; Pelton 1997, 549). Thus, more children may enter the system in the coming years.

The goals of welfare reform and the potential results for children in kinship care are not congruent. The perceived aims of the new policies are to make welfare recipients more responsible for themselves (and their families) and to provide permanency for children in foster care. However, time limits on AFDC payments to parents erect obstacles for individuals previously able to care for their own children with financial assistance, possibly forcing them to place their child with a relative. In addition, mandated adoption proceedings within 18 months of foster care may be prematurely terminating the parental rights of individuals who are willing to care for their children, but who are financially unable to do so. In contrast to the "family values" mind-set of the current administration, new welfare policies, though well intended, may be pushing some children away from their families.

This greater push to terminate parental rights and move these children quickly into adoption presents even more challenges. This chapter examines the realities of adoption for children currently in the foster care system.

## ❏ SPECIAL NEEDS ADOPTIONS

The term "special needs adoptions" generally refers to the adoptive placement of older children, sibling groups, children of color, and children with physical, emotional, or mental problems (Rosenthal 1993; McRoy 1999a). Many of these children who are in the nation's foster care system have been sexually or physically abused and/or neglected by their birth parents and are in out-of-home care.

Adoption terminates parental rights and responsibilities of a birth family and establishes a new legal parent-child relationship with adoptive parents (Horejsi 1996). This permanency option is a form of substitute parenting typically used when a child cannot be returned to his or her family of origin (McDaniel, Merkel-Holguin, and Brittain 1997). In 1997, the Adoption and Safe Families Act (ASFA) (discussed in chapter 1) was passed to expedite permanency decisions by allowing for simultaneous reunification and adoption plans once a child enters care; the Act also reauthorizes funding and expands provisions for family preservation and support services, including time-limited reunification services and adoption promotion and support. President Clinton set a goal that by 2002, 54,000 waiting foster children would be placed in adoption annually (PL 105-89, Adoption and Safe Families Act of 1997).

Adoption itself presents challenges for a child and family. Children placed for adoption bring a history of genetic and psychological ties, experiences, and past relationships to the adoptive family. Many times children come to the adoption after experiencing abuse and neglect, and several separations and losses while in foster care; children may also blame themselves for their placement. They may exhibit mental, physical, emotional, and behavioral problems (Steinhauer 1991). The experience of child maltreatment or of being removed from one's family of origin and placement, as well as experiences while in care, represent significant risk factors for potential maladaptive behavior. The older the child, the greater the likelihood of experiencing a longer period of maltreatment and/or longer and/or multiple placements in out-of-home care (Garland et al. 1996).

As the child grows in the adoptive home, he/she will continually have to adjust to his/her understanding of the reasons for adoption and to the new environment. Families as well must adjust to not having early parenting experiences with the child and the unique challenges of parenting a child born to another set of parents who has a different history and genetic background (McDaniel, Merkel-Holguin, and Brittain 1997, 9).

Although most adoptions are successful, studies on adoption disruptions have indicated a rate of 21 percent for children ten or older at the time of placement (Barth et al. 1988). Others have reported a rate of 47 percent for children 12 and older (Boyne et al. 1982).

Adoption can be a positive outcome for many children who cannot return to their families. However, adoption remains elusive for many of these special needs children. As disproportionately high numbers of these children are African American, this chapter focuses on the placement options being utilized for this population.

## ❑ ADOPTION OPTIONS FOR AFRICAN AMERICAN CHILDREN

*Informal Adoptions.* According to U.S. Census Bureau data, in all ethnic groups at all socioeconomic levels, grandparents are serving as parents; this pattern is particularly prevalent in the African American population (Boston Aging Concerns Young & Old Inc. 1994). Of the 1 million African American children currently living with grandparents or other relatives, 80 percent are informally adopted by these kin (Hill 1997). Historically, this phenomenon can be attributed to strong kinship links and the traditional practice within the African American community of informal adoption by the extended family. The African American kin network has been credited as being instrumental in the survival and advancement of African Americans (e.g., Hill 1977; Brody and Stoneman 1992) by providing a stress-absorbing system in times of trouble, as well as an important source of emotional and instrumental support (Minkler, Roe, and Robertson-Beckley 1994). Moreover, Hill (1977, 1) states:

> One of the most vital functions that this strong kinship network has performed is the informal absorption or "adoption" of children. During slavery, for example, thousands of children of slave parents, who had been sold as chattel, were often reared by elderly relatives who served as a major source of stability and fortitude for many black families.

Examining the ecological network following emancipation, child welfare services reunited former slave children with their parents, but African American children were often excluded from the developing foster care system as well as from the primarily white charity organization societies and settlement houses. As a response, African American neighborhoods created their own agencies (Turner Hogan and Siu 1988). Thus, the precedent of the African American community caring for its own family members was maintained.

As recently as the late 1980s, African American children continued to face the problems of having less access to the more costly social services (such as group homes and residential treatment), spending longer time in foster care, waiting as much as 2.5 times longer for adoptive placements, and being overrepresented in abuse and neglect reports (Turner Hogan and Siu 1988). As a solution, Scannapieco and Jackson (1996) suggest that kinship care, both formal and informal, is the current response of the African American community in order to preserve families facing the present obstacles of poverty, the AIDS epidemic, increased reports of child abuse and neglect, and cutbacks in social programs. With the goals of permanence and continuity for children in mind, Gray and Nybell (1990) suggest that agencies and policy makers should explore the development of policies that support this cultural tradition.

*Formal Inracial Adoptions.* African American children who are free for adoption often wait longer than white children for placement, as traditional public and private agencies sometimes have difficulty recruiting and retaining African American families (McRoy, Oglesby, and Grape 1997). African American families are often blamed for their failure to adopt children whereas in reality many are being screened out of the process. According to the National Urban League study of 800 African American families who applied nationwide to become adoptive parents, only two were approved for adoption. The national average for approval is 10 percent (*National Association of Social Workers News* 1984).

One of the reasons traditional adoption agency staff may not have been successful in recruiting these interested families is due to the lack of minority staff. According to the National Child Welfare Training Center, 78 percent of adoption workers are white, 80 percent of supervisors are white, and most have not received cultural sensitivity training and practice with African American families (Vinokur-Kaplan and Hartman 1986).

Moreover, although a study by the North American Council on Adoptable Children (NACAC) has reported that minority specializing adoption programs are more likely to make successful adoptive placements of African American children than traditional programs, most public and private agencies have been reluctant to establish specialized programs (McKenzie 1993). Minority specializing agencies place 94 percent of their African American children inracially, while traditional agencies place only 51 percent of their children inracially (North American Council on Adoptable Children 1993; Simon, Altstein, and Melli 1994).

According to a National Urban League African American Pulse survey, about 3 million African American household heads have expressed an interest in formally adopting (Hill 1993). Mason and Williams (1985) found that when family composition, income, and age are controlled, African American families actually adopt at four times the rate of white families.

The Child Welfare League of America acknowledged that African American families can be found for infants, preschoolers, and school-age African American children (Sullivan 1994). However, two recent studies of minority adoptions have reported barriers to African American families adopting. Rodriguez and Meyer (1990) found agency policies and lack of minority staff to be barriers and noted that successful agencies used single parents as adoptive resources, had culturally competent staff, utilized subsidies, and educated minority communities about adoption. Similarly, the North American Council on Adoptable Children (1991) found lack of minority staff, agency fees, inflexible standards, and institutional/systemic racism to be barriers to same-race placements.

*Transracial Adoptions.* The merits of transracial placements have been hotly debated in the research literature as well as in public forums for years. Most, however, conclude that same-race placements are preferable (McRoy 1994). However, given the number of African American children in the system needing placement, the growing number of white families seeking to adopt, and traditional adoption agencies' limited success in finding African American families, many agencies have encouraged white families to consider adopting transracially (McRoy, Oglesby, and Grape 1997; McRoy 1989).

In 1987, Simon and Altstein reported that approximately 2 million white couples were seeking to adopt, yet there were very few white infants available for adoption. As the supply of white infants is limited, and the demand is high, agencies have very stringent criteria for white families seeking healthy white infants. Some white families have resigned themselves to becoming foster parents and some maintain the hope that they may be able to adopt one day.

Prior to 1994, most agencies generally placed children in racially matched adoptive families. However, the large supply of African American children needing foster care and the large supply of white foster families led many agencies to place African American children in white foster families. As many of these foster placements involved African American infants or young children, white foster parents often became very attached to the children in their care and sought to adopt. There have been complex legal battles between white foster families who seek to adopt very young African American children in their care and state or private agencies seeking to place these children for adoption with either African American adoptive families or with extended kin. The publicity associated with these cases, along with the growing number of African American children in the child welfare system, and delays in finding adoptive families for African American children, were major factors leading toward the passage of legislation to eliminate barriers to transracial adoptions.

In 1994, Congress passed the Multiethnic Placement Act (MEPA, PL 103-382), which prohibits any foster care or adoption agency or entity that receives federal financial assistance from denying a placement solely on the basis of race, but allows for consideration of the cultural, ethnic, or racial background of the child and the capacity of the foster parents to meet the needs of a child of this background (McRoy and Hall 1995). In 1996, the Act was amended by the provisions for Removal of Barriers to Interethnic Adoption (IEP) as part of the Small Business Job Protection Act (PL 104-188). This amendment clarified that "discrimination is not to be tolerated" and strengthened compliance and enforcement procedures, including withholding of federal funds if a state or other entity was in violation of the law. This legislation was designed to remove barriers to permanency by decreasing the wait for children in the system, facilitating recruitment and retention of families, and eliminating discrimination in adoption decision-making (Hollinger 1998). According to the law, "agencies can no longer assume that children have needs related to their race, color, or national origin" (Hollinger 1998, 2). As mentioned earlier in this chapter, many believe that this legislation, which protects the practice of transracial adoption, will truly reduce the number of African American children in foster care.

In reality, however, the Multiethnic Placement Act will probably enable only a small number of white families to adopt minority foster children who have been in their homes since infancy. It is important to reiterate that the actual number of transracial placements is very small (1% of adoptions in 1987 were transracial placements) (Stolley 1993), and there are no reliable data to suggest that there is a significant demand by white families for African American children (Courtney 1997a). According to the National Health Interview Survey, adoptions of African American children by white parents account for only about 1 percent of all adoptions (Stolley 1993). It is estimated that transracial adoptions account for only about 1,000 to 2,000 placements of African American children each year (Brooks 1991), and that the majority of white families are seeking to adopt infants. As most waiting children are older, transracial adoptions will have no significant impact on the growing number of children in out-of-home care (*The Economist* 1994).

It is also important to note that the Multiethnic Placement Act will probably serve as a greater barrier for African American families adopting as racial matching can no longer be considered a priority in placing children. (Same-race placements of white children have continued.) In fact, adoption workers now may be subject to civil liability suits if their recommendation to place an African American child within race is not well documented and supported (Alexander and Curtis 1996). In Texas, workers can lose their jobs if they delay or deny a placement for the purposes of racial matching (McRoy, Oglesby, and Grape 1997). Such laws not only prevent workers from finding families that are most like the family, community, and culture from which the child came, they are likely to discourage African American families from adopting and lead to more African American children lingering in the system.

## ❏ CONCLUSION

Adoption remains an elusive option for many children in the system, especially African American children. Although legislative initiatives have been undertaken to promote transracial placements, these policies will not solve the problem of permanence for growing numbers of children. Systemic barriers including disparate treatment of children have led to many of these children languishing in care. Traditional adoption agencies have not followed the direction of minority specializing agencies who have been successful in placing African American children within African American families. There are also large numbers of white and minority older children that need to be targeted for placement services. The reality is that many prospective adopters are seeking infants and young children. In order to address the problem of older children in the system, we must be creative in considering alternative options for children, including kinship care and expanded family preservation services, to enable many of these children to remain within their own families. The following chapter will address the needs for expanded options for children in the new millennium.

# CHAPTER FIVE

# Family Preservation in the New Millennium

Historically, child welfare practices and policies in the United States have been developed in response to problems experienced primarily by impoverished families and children. Current solutions tend to provide a temporary fix for symptoms of the problem (e.g., substance abuse, child abuse, and child neglect) rather than solving the underlying problem—poverty. These solutions have primarily involved protecting the children by removing them from their biological families and placing them in foster families for which financial and support services are provided. While in foster care, children can experience multiple placements, can sometimes be victims of abuse, and some are temporarily or permanently reunited with their birth families. Some children are placed permanently with adoptive families, which in some cases are of a different cultural and ethnic background than the child's family of origin.

Confounding these issues further are recent efforts to "reform" welfare programs by cutting entitlements, tightening eligibility requirements, restricting the length of time one can receive benefits, and increasing work and educational participation requirements (Gleeson 1996). Interestingly, while these policy reforms may reduce welfare rolls in one arena, in another arena, they may actually have quite a different effect than intended.

As pointed out by Woodworth (1996), recent changes in welfare policy may specifically have an adverse effect on the numbers of grandparents caring for grandchildren. Related to the newly imposed five-year limits to welfare, Woodworth (1996, 626) considers that the answer to the question,

"Where do the children go if their parents cannot afford to care for them?" will most likely be, "To live with their grandparents." As a result, children may be coming off AFDC support, only to be added to the foster care rolls in formal kinship care. For years, no financial support was given to members of extended families who wished to provide care for their kin. Policies have changed and now sometimes these kin care providers can qualify for foster care payments.

Moreover, in recent years, legislation has been passed that has called for services to preserve more birth families through the temporary provision of relatively low-cost concrete and support services. Research results on these programs have demonstrated that family preservation services have reduced the likelihood of out-of-home placements. Regardless, reports of child fatalities occurring in families in which family preservation services had been offered have led some to blame family preservation programs. For example, according to Gelles (1996b, 4):

> The fact that nearly half of all the children killed by their caretakers are killed after the children or their families have come to the attention of the child welfare system is compelling evidence that the goal of preserving families can lead to the death or preventable injury of children.

Instead of blaming programs or policies for problems, we need to look at the entire system of child welfare services and identify needed changes. We must acknowledge that the system has not always protected the children or found ways to help families provide for the well-being of their children, or, when necessary, found appropriate placements for children. In many cases, failure to implement programs, lack of sufficient resources to effectively support the programs and families, and/or inadequate resources to train the workers in conducting good assessments to determine which children are at risk of harm may have led to negative outcomes, not the programs themselves. Moreover, child fatalities occurred long before family preservation services were fully operational. For example, in 1988, nearly 1 million children were abused or neglected in this country; there were about 1,100 fatalities. Most of the latter cases had never been reported to child protective services (U.S. Department of Health and Human Services 1998).

Instead of viewing family preservation and child protective services as opposites, they should be viewed as part of a continuum of necessary child welfare services. In this chapter, issues associated with the provision of family preservation, foster care, kinship care, and adoption will be discussed, with particular attention given to the problems faced by African

American children in the child welfare system. This chapter addresses each of these issues and presents recommendations for addressing the protection and care of children in the new millennium.

*Family Preservation.* The ideal means of achieving permanency for children is providing supportive, financial, and concrete services for their own families to enable them to remain at home. Ronnau and Marlow (1993, 40) have suggested that family preservation programs base their services on the following beliefs:

- People of all ages can best develop and their lives be enhanced, with few exceptions, by remaining with their family or relying on their family as an important resource.
- The family members' ethnic, cultural, and religious background and values, and community ties, are important resources to be used in the helping process.
- The definition of "family" is varied, and each family should be approached as a unique system.
- Policies at the local, state, and national levels should be formulated to strengthen, empower, and support families.
- Families have the potential to change, and most troubled families want to do so (Ronnau and Sallee 1993).

If we truly believe that most families, if given support, can safely raise their own children, then we need to help preserve these families, rather than take children from the poor and give financial assistance to foster families to raise them, or place them with more affluent families through adoption. The unequal provision of family preservation services to African American families as well as the temporary nature of concrete services offered through family preservation are among the current challenges to this program. Each is discussed below.

In 1992, there were 2,855,691 children who were reported as abused and neglected. Slightly over 27 percent of those were African American (Children's Defense Fund 1995). Recent studies have shown that minority families, particularly African American families, are more likely than other families to be reported for abuse and neglect. For example, Hampton (1986) found that African American children were more likely to be reported to child protective services as alleged victims of abuse than white children, and Turbett and O'Toole (1980, cited in Hampton 1986) demonstrated that a fictitious child is 33 percent more likely to be a suspected victim of abuse if the evaluating physician believes the child is African American.

Moreover, as mentioned earlier, although African American children comprise only 15 percent of the total U.S. child population, 44 percent of African American children live in poverty (Children's Defense Fund 1996). A relationship has been found between poverty and likelihood of a child being removed and placed in out-of-home care (Pelton 1989; Lindsey 1991). It follows that African American children are much more likely to be removed from their families and placed in care.

Moreover, several researchers—Pinderhughes (1991), Morisey (1990), and Denby et al. (1998)—have reported that family preservation services are often not targeted to African American families. Morisey (1990) noted that white workers may view African American families as stereotypically dysfunctional and may reserve preservation services for more "treatable" populations. Similarly, Hodges (1991) suggested that racist attitudes and lack of understanding about ethnic family issues contribute to placement decisions. Denby and Alford (1995) reported that workers in their sample felt that targeting services to African American clients might be considered "an affirmative action type of process" and was therefore not done. Similarly, Schuerman et al. (1992b) and Rossi (1992) noted that families who were viewed by workers as most likely to benefit from services received them and those whose children were considered at greater risk for placement did not always receive them.

Nelson and Landsman (1991) found that the majority of families in their nationwide study of five family preservation programs had incomes of less than $10,000. It is not surprising that studies of family preservation outcomes have found a relationship between the provision of concrete services and effectiveness of services. For example, according to Berry (1992), families in her study that made the greatest gain in skills and the families that remained intact had been provided with concrete services. This suggests that many of the problems families faced that may have led to child removal stemmed from lack of adequate income resources for basic necessities such as food, clothing, and housing. However, once the temporary intervention is over, it sometimes becomes difficult to avoid out-of-home placement. If families are successful in avoiding placement and families are kept together, they are typically preserved in poverty (Eamon 1994). Until we address the high child poverty rates in this country through social legislation that preserves families through the provision of adequate income, temporary fixes will continue to be found wanting.

*Kinship Care.* With the declining number of traditional foster families and growing number of children needing placement, kinship care is becoming much more of a formalized response to the need (see chapter 3).

Between 400,000 to 500,000 children are in kinship care arrangements and the majority of these children are African American (Berrick et al. 1994; Dubowitz 1990; Iglehart 1994; Task Force on Permanency Planning for Foster Children 1990). In some large urban areas such as New York City, there are more children in kinship care than in traditional foster care. This traditional form of family caregiving in African American communities, which has recently been formalized and sanctioned by child welfare services, needs to be studied. Services should be culturally appropriate and acknowledge the cultural and familial strengths within the African American community (Scannapieco and Jackson 1996).

Studies on permanency goals of children in kinship placements have revealed that most kinship care providers are not interested in legal adoption, even though the child will probably never return to the birth parents (Thornton 1991). As one kin care provider in Thornton's study stated: "I'm helping out because their parents are unable to care for them. These children have parents and I want them to know this. Adoption is unnecessary: We are already a family!" (Thornton 1991, 597).

Since adoption is not a goal in many of these placements, cities and states will have to find a way to fund these programs in order to continue payments for a long period of time and to provide for administrative expenses. Some locales are considering giving kin care providers status as guardians under which they would receive stipends for children in care but supervision would be curtailed (Thornton 1991). As many of the kin caregivers are single, economically disadvantaged women of color (Berrick et al. 1994; Thornton 1991), service providers will need to be culturally competent and find ways to support and strengthen these informal helping systems (Gleeson, O'Donnell, and Bonecutter 1997). As Brown and Bailey-Etta (1997, 76) reported:

> Kinship care arrangements should not be pursued by child welfare agencies as a cost-effective way to avoid providing supportive services to children and families in need. African American children in kinship care tend to receive fewer services than do children in non-relative family foster care, and fewer services than their Caucasian counterparts in kinship care.

Efforts should be made to safeguard the rights of kin care providers, and to ensure adequate funding, supervision, and supportive services to these families to prevent a two-tiered system of foster care in the United States—one white with resources and state support and another that is urban, minority, and without resources (Hegar and Scannapieco 1999). Kinship care practice should involve members of the kinship network in all aspects of the case, including assessment, decision-making, and implementing a service plan (Gleeson 1995). Such programs must recognize the resilient nature of the African American family and services should be directed toward the child, biological parents, and kin caregivers (Scannapieco and Jackson 1996).

## ❑ RECOMMENDATIONS

Family preservation services will be needed more than ever in the new millennium. However, they need to be funded sufficiently so that families can actually be helped beyond a temporary fix. Currently, some services only delay out-of-home placement—once services are curtailed, the family plummets back into poverty and again lacks the few concrete resources that temporarily reduced the problem.

Suggestions for modifying services are as follows:

- Adapt family preservation programs and kinship services to incorporate the diverse, rich cultural heritage and support networks in African American communities. This may prove helpful in reducing the number of children who enter the system (Carter 1997).
- Since resources are often limited, family preservation services can be extended by linking with the African American church and the strengths of the community. Concrete services such as food and clothing as well as natural helping networks such as child care providers within the African American community can connect with the family and serve as useful components of family preservation services (Carter 1997).
- Family preservation services need to be a part of a continuum of services for families. All people need family connections, but if this cannot be accomplished through family preservation or kinship care, we should consider adoption, which comes closest to family connectedness and provides permanence (Forsythe 1989).
- Adequate assessments of families require physicians, counselors, educators, psychologists, and so on. A team of professionals should be involved in assessing families and designing intervention strategies to improve family functioning. Assessments should focus on strengths of the family.

- Services need to be comprehensive and longer term. Follow-up visits should continue at least a year after termination. Intervention strategies should be based on theory as well as proven strategies that work.
- Each family may need a specific type of service depending on unique needs and strengths. Services should be designed accordingly (Wells and Tracy 1996).
- Longitudinal research is needed to assess families' progress over time and to assess the most effective services. Qualitative case studies as well as quantitative studies are needed.

## ❏ IMPLICATIONS FOR THE FUTURE

Family preservation services have been found to be very effective for many families and can keep children out of the child welfare system. They have been found to improve family functioning, if these service providers emphasize family strengths and empowerment, provide concrete services, and are focused on the developmental needs of each child and family. The intervention should be linked to theoretical models of child maltreatment (National Research Council 1993), be culturally competent (Denby and Alford 1995), and focus on preventing the recurrence of abuse and neglect (Wells and Tracy 1996). Moreover, family preservation should extend beyond child welfare services and should be the mission of other organizations including mental health, health, juvenile justice, education, services to elderly, among others (Warsh, Pine, and Maluccio 1995).

Family preservation does not replace foster care and adoption, as some children will be in families that cannot be preserved and will need these services. However, it is clear from the research presented in this book that family preservation can be a very effective tool and workers should be trained in better assessing families to determine when supportive services can be used to obviate the need for child removal.

Nevertheless, we still must find ways to attack two more central problems—poverty and funding out-of-home care. As long as welfare reform efforts strip families of support, and fiscal incentives remain for out-of-home care, we will continue to see significant growth in the number of poor children living away from their families in out-of-home care. Moreover, as long as we believe that transracial placements represent the panacea for children of color in the child welfare system and fail to address the systemic barriers to same-race adoptions and the inequities in service provision to African American children and families, we will continue to see disproportionately high numbers of African American children in out-of-home care.

# PART TWO

# Howard Altstein
*Family Preservation/Adoption:*
*Misplaced Hope versus What Works*

# CHAPTER SIX

# Family Preservation: What Does the Research Say?

A question that arose early in the nation's struggle to develop an effective child welfare system is in large part similar to the one being discussed in this monograph. In the early twentieth century, the question was whether foster care or orphanages were better or more effective. At that time one variant of foster care was to send groups of needy children to farm families in the Midwest. As the decades passed, social workers, public officials, and others would ask: How effective is foster care? How and when should it be used? How can children be kept out of it? What are the alternatives to foster care? At the end of the twentieth century, we had no definitive answers. In this and subsequent chapters the initial question has been somewhat reframed to: What is the empirical evidence for continuing support for family preservation (and kinship care) programs? Family preservation is a broad concept with several programmatic designs. But all strategies share a common outcome, the preservation of the family unit by preventing a child's entry into foster care.

As a society we have been very inventive in attempting to solve the problem of what to do with children who for reasons not of their own making cannot remain with their birth families. Over the years we have created programs such as foster care and its variants (e.g., subsidized foster care), group homes, kinship care, adoption and its variants, orphanages (revisited), concurrent planning, and the topic of this book, family preservation. All have champions and detractors. All have theories explaining why they should be effective and all have research supporting, to some degree, their effectiveness.

But in the view of this writer, adoption is the one practice with a convincing body of evidence that demonstrates greater effectiveness than other practices. But adoption is not a one-size-fits-all solution, nor is it without risk. All other efforts at family rehabilitation must be exhausted before adoption is defined as the practice of choice. Adoption is a final act; it rests on a child's being legally available for adoption. In other words, the birth parent(s)' parental rights must be legally severed from the child. The process is known as termination of parental rights and it is a drastic, last resort decision for any court to make.

Society has given the field of social work (for the most part) the heavy responsibility of deciding a troubled child's future. Our personal and therefore biased penchants notwithstanding, the caveat we as social workers must follow is to ground our professional behavior on what has been empirically demonstrated as longitudinally effective by well-conceptualized research designs. It is not sufficient to bemoan the fact that foster care has not solved our nation's child care crisis after almost a century. Our actions, and what separates us from our ascientific past, must be guided by data. Professional conduct cannot be driven by what we would wish would happen, nor what our intuition tells us should happen, but rather by what has been objectively demonstrated. We have no other choice. Failure to operationalize into social work practice what has been empirically demonstrated as in a child's best interests is to deny social work's attempts to develop "scientific practice." No profession, including social work, can support interventions that are not sustained by strong empirical evidence. Politics, ideology, and rhetoric have no place in deciding what is in any child's best interest.

The pillars of our child welfare system are known but worth repeating. Permanency plans should (1) do no harm, (2) conform to the "best interest" axiom, (3) be the least restrictive, and (4) promote permanence. In essence, this book is about these four principles, and allows for two points of view. The perspective taken in this section will be to examine the extent to which family preservation services are supported by credible research designs yielding reasonable enough data to support the social work profession's continued faith in their viability.

There will be no rush to judgment in addressing the extent to which family preservation has been shown to be effective. These programs were designed and trumpeted about with an enormous amount of hope. No one should disparage such efforts. At the risk of sounding melodramatic, the lives of hundreds of thousands of our nation's children ride on the success of these programs. If the children's parents and extended families are calculated into this human equation, then the success or failure of family preservation programs affects the lives of literally millions of people. For the most part, families targeted for family preservation interventions are our society's most needy, such as intergenerational recipients of various types of welfare assistance from federal, state, and local social service organizations. All social workers want family preservation to work, that is, to enable problematic families to reach adequate levels of well-being where their children could be raised in nurturing environments without the threat of removal.

Two models of family-focused programs exist that at times are confused. One is known as family support, and the other as family preservation. Both target the family unit as "the client." But family support programs are designed to deal with families experiencing what Thomas Szasz (1974) would refer to as "problems of everyday living" (e.g., child-rearing difficulties).

Family preservation services, on the other hand, deal with families whose difficulties are much more pronounced, dysfunctional, severe, and even pathologic. In some cases, these are families that have been known to the social welfare and mental health systems across generations. For the majority of these families, the goal is either to prevent a child's removal into foster care, or to prepare the ground for a child's return from foster care. In cases where neither goal is possible—that is, where the family is dysfunctional to the point that a child's safety would be in danger if s/he remained or returned from foster care—termination of parental rights is sought (Fraser, Nelson, and Rivard 1997; Pecora, Fraser, and Nelson 1995). It is in these multi-problem families that one reads of the now too common tragedies of children brutally abused, even killed, because on the basis of a social worker's evaluation, they were either left with their pathologic family in the name of family preservation or returned from foster care, in the name of "family reunification."

Families eligible for family preservation are in all likelihood those who will be the most affected by the new welfare reform statute known as the 1996 Personal Responsibility and Work Opportunity Reconciliation Act (PRA). For these families, and especially their children, the proverbial clock is ticking. Unless a family is placed in the "hardship" category, PRA allows for a total of 60 months of lifetime assistance. Only 20 percent of a state's "customers" (known as welfare recipients or clients prior to PRA) may be placed in this category. After that, families are no longer eligible for most federally supported social services. The rationale for the development of family preservation services was straightforward: to reduce the large number of children entering an already overburdened foster care system. Specifically, family preservation services are defined as follows:

> . . . short-term, intensive, crisis intervention services delivered in a family's home. The purpose is to safely prevent the unnecessary placement of children who are at imminent risk of removal due to child abuse, neglect, juvenile delinquency, status offenses, emotional problems or trouble in school.

> Specially trained caseworkers handle only two or three cases at a time, allowing them to monitor families with an intensity that provides excellent assurance of safety for all concerned. The intervention lasts only four to six weeks. (Forsythe 1992, 41)

The above definition has proven to be more viable in theory than in practice. Upon examining family preservation designs, several theories and their derivative approaches directing interventions were found. Most, if not all, interventions appear to be based on the Homebuilders model of Intensive Family Preservation Services (IFPS). According to Bath and Haapala (1993, 213), the prototypic IFPS is

> . . . designed to prevent the unnecessary placement of children out of their homes while at the same time ensuring their safety. This is achieved through the provision of a mix of intensive therapeutic and support services tailored to the needs of families in crisis. Intervention is typically intensive in client contact yet limited to four to six weeks in duration.

> The model is the most widely disseminated and replicated one in the FPS [family-based services] field.

Kinney, Haapala, and Booth (1991, 27) found several commonalities unique to Homebuilders IFPS. For example, they all tend to focus on

> an ecological approach, services provided in the natural environment, intensive ("whatever it takes") services, small caseloads (two to five), short-term intervention, single counselor with team back-up, emphasis on staff training and skill development, goal orientation and twenty-four-hour availability.

Using the dual theoretical concepts inherent in ecological and empowerment models, intensive family preservation strategies attempt to understand the factors associated with a family's dysfunction and how these dysfunctional patterns can be altered.

> Empowerment-based practice stresses mastery of the environment, self-determination and a recognition of the social forces that negatively affect one's life. (Gibson 1993, 389)

Homebuilders IFPS attempt to minimize the social worker's influence and control over clients by emphasizing family strengths rather than dysfunctions. By structuring intervention in this manner, the social worker assumes the role of advocate and not expert. Through the use of these strategies in Homebuilders intensive family preservation models, social workers encourage families to understand and change dysfunctional behaviors in order to reduce chances of abuse or neglect (Bath and Haapala 1993). Family preservation designs can have a broad spectrum of community-based activities but in general, the purpose is to reach families before child abuse or neglect occurs.

In addition to presenting accumulated evidence indicating that most family preservation designs have not for the most part achieved their primary goal of reducing or eliminating the likelihood that children would enter foster care (or other temporary placements), evidence is presented in the following chapters about effective strategies, namely adoption, and particularly transracial adoption (TRA). A large amount of literature exists supporting the long-term benefits of any type of adoption, ranging from traditional heterosexual two-parent inracial adoption (IRA) of nondisabled children, to single-parent adoption of handicapped children, to adoption of one child and of sibling groups.

Even when special needs children are involved, adoption works. To quote respected adoption investigators Rosenthal and Groze from their 1992 study:

> Special-needs adoption works. Adoption workers know this from their own practice . . . for almost all children who cannot return to their biological families, adoption is the best plan. (218)

The above statement was reinforced in Groze and Rosenthal's (1996) longitudinal study of families who successfully adopted special needs children.

In the following section, research on family preservation programs is examined with the aim of determining whether the strategy is effective, that is, whether it works or achieves what its supporters want it to achieve. In brief, do data exist indicating that these strategies prevent a child's entry into foster care or restore families to a level of functioning whereby their children can be returned from foster care?

To paraphrase a contemporary idiom, I will "follow the (evaluative) data" on family preservation programs and then examine them in light of the alternative, adoption. The following is not an exhaustive review of the literature on family preservation programs, but instead is limited to works that test the model via research designs yielding data.

In this chapter, PL 104-193, the Personal Responsibility and Work Opportunity Reconciliation Act of 1996, is also discussed in terms of its possible influence on family preservation interventions. Chapter 8 is dedicated to a broader discussion of PL 105-89, the Adoption and Safe Families Act of 1997, and PL 104-188, the Multiethnic Placement Act (MEPA) of 1996.

## ❑ DISCUSSION AND LITERATURE REVIEW OF FAMILY PRESERVATION PROGRAMS

"Effectiveness" is at times an elusive and difficult concept to operationalize, especially in social work, the profession most often correctly identified with family preservation programming. What may seem not successful or effective at a given time may in the long term have some ameliorative effect. But, in most if not practically all cases, investigators do not have the luxury of time and resources to conduct longitudinal studies. Even if they did and positive results were found in the long term, could family preservation efforts take credit for the results, or were other factors equally or more important?

Effectiveness is best demonstrated through the classic experimental design where two similar groups (of families) are assembled, with one receiving in this case family preservation intervention and the other receiving traditional intervention(s) or no services. At the end of a given period, both groups are examined to determine whether predicted results were achieved. This is a simplistic illustration of the type of design necessary to demonstrate effectiveness. A review of literature revealed that practically no definitive data exist suggesting that family preservation works, that indeed these efforts actually made a real difference in the lives of families and prevented a child's removal from the home.

One of the tenets of modern social work is that most individuals and families, when provided with necessary psychosocial supports, can be rehabilitated in various degrees to the extent that they achieve some level of functioning whereby they contribute to the social good. But child welfare practitioners also recognize, however reluctantly, that not all families are capable of rehabilitation, despite all the best intentions and, at times, heroic social service interventions. Time does not favor children whose families are experiencing difficulty. Time does not favor children who are in the institutionalized holding pattern we call foster care. Time does not favor children experiencing transience. Time does not favor children who rapidly develop and mature. One of the pillars of virtually all variants of family preservation is to prevent a child's permanent removal from the birth family. To accomplish this laudable outcome—in other words, to sufficiently stabilize a family whereby adults are capable of providing a nurturing environment for their children, free from neglect and abuse—intensive services of many types are provided for a finite period of time. Family preservation was designed to achieve this "homeostasis," a term much used in social work to describe a stable family environment.

The reasons for many children's removal from their birth families into foster care are physical/sexual abuse and neglect, with parental substance abuse the precipitating factor in the majority of cases (Azzi-Lessing and Olsen 1996; Besharov 1996b; CWLA 1992; Courtney 1994; Dore, Doris, and Wright, 1995; Slaught 1993; Tracy 1994). Some suggest that parental substance abuse is responsible for a staggering 90 percent of all placements into foster care (Jaudes, Ekwo, and Voorhis 1995). Many in the field also argue that substance abuse is a chronic condition, a condition the child welfare establishment is ill-equipped to remediate (Besharov 1996b).

A reexamination of both theory and intervention strategies upon which family preservation practice rests is suggested by many who cite evidence that most substance abusing parents are usually unable in the short or long term to provide the type of nurturing milieu their children require for healthy development (Besharov 1996b; Curtis and McCoullough 1991; Tracy 1994). Their dependency on drugs and alcohol not only is the reason children are removed but complicates efforts at reunification.

When one examines the history of the nation's efforts to find solutions to the problem of parentless children, what we often see are policies and practices that are not driven by research data. What we have instead are programs reflecting the social and political zeitgeist of the time. From placing parentless children on trains heading west to be raised in the "healthy environment of the farm" (actually a form of indenture) to an emphasis on attempting to keep families together, our solutions have rested on the social norms of the times. Family preservation programs are reflections of U.S. culture as we enter the twenty-first century, wherein the value of family life is strongly emphasized, almost as a panacea for all social ills.

But the politically incorrect question that must be asked is: When is a point of diminishing returns reached? In other words, is there a time when family preservation social workers should realize that no amount of intervention, no matter how well meaning and conceived, intensive and thorough, will be able to render a given family capable of providing adequate and nurturing care for its children? At what point must social workers recognize that the likelihood such families will be able to reinvent themselves into contributing members of their communities is very slight? For the most part, despite much research, we do not possess appropriate evaluative models to declare when that level has been reached and it's time to go to the next step of beginning termination of parental rights proceedings as now called for by federal statute.

Termination of parental rights proceedings are central to family preservation alternatives. If instituted in a timely fashion, they should allow for the rescue of children from destructive environments. Terminating parental rights is also a major part of PL 105-89, the Adoption and Safe Families Act of 1997. This statute requires that termination of parental rights proceedings begin if a child has been in foster care for 15 of the previous 22 months. Equally important, this legislation reduces from 18 to 12 months the length of time available to design a permanency plan.

The notion of family preservation can be dated to passage of PL 96-272, the Adoption Assistance and Child Welfare Act of 1980. Among other mandates, this statute called for social workers to make "reasonable efforts" in keeping families together, thereby (hopefully) preventing the likely removal of children to foster care. The ambiguousness of the term "reasonable efforts" in practice is one of two factors leading to family preservation's lack of success. The other is that since passage of PL 96-272, there is a fundamental discrepancy between a child's best interest and simultaneously attempting to either keep that child with the dysfunctional family or working toward the child's return (from foster care) to the family. In the words of Gelles (1996a, 84):

> The problem is not simply that resources are lacking, but that the central mission of child welfare agencies, preserving families, does not work and places many children at significant risk of continued injury and death.

In the late 1980s, increases in drug use, homelessness, and poverty resulted in dramatic increases in rates of child abuse and neglect. These events drove the number of children entering and remaining in foster care upward. In attempting to improve services for children and their families as well as reducing foster care costs, states began to rethink their approaches to child welfare. Rather than wait until families reached the crisis stage, states began to focus more on early intervention and provision of preventive services designed to strengthen and support families. Simply put, this was the beginning of what came to be known as family preservation services.

But, despite all efforts, by the early 1990s the U.S. child welfare system was overwhelmed by the needs of an increasing number of at-risk families and children. States started to lobby for more federal dollars to supplement their own and federally funded programs. In order to assist states in providing services designed to support families and help keep them together (thereby reducing foster care costs), Congress enacted legislation (Family Preservation and Support Services Program) as part of PL 103-66, the Omnibus Budget Reconciliation Act of 1993. A total of $930 million was allocated to states over a five-year period, no less than 25 percent of which was specifically earmarked for family preservation services.

Originally, family preservation interventions targeted families already in crisis, whose children in all likelihood would otherwise be removed from their homes. These services were to serve families where child abuse or neglect had occurred or where children were identified as representing a danger to themselves or others. These families risked having their children temporarily or permanently placed outside the home in foster care, juvenile detention, or mental health facilities. Most family preservation programs provided specific services designed to fit the family's needs to help eliminate the underlying causes of dysfunction, such as family counseling and training in parenting skills. The intensity, duration, and packaging of services distinguished these programs from the traditional delivery of child welfare services, which also have the goal of placement prevention and family reunification.

Although family preservation strategies vary, the most popular design as mentioned earlier derives from the Homebuilders prototype. Using an intensive crisis intervention model, child welfare workers typically carry small caseloads of less than five families at a time and are available to families on a 24-hour basis for four to six weeks. Traditional models call for child welfare workers to carry caseloads of up to scores of families with limited contacts for extended periods of time.

Despite the good intentions of the Homebuilders strategy, Welles (1994, 475), an observer of family preservation programs, reported the following:

[R]esearch shows that a high proportion of families served by Homebuilders-type programs improve their functioning and have children who remain out of placement. It is important to note here, however, that it cannot be inferred that the programs prevented the placement of children because it is uncertain that they would have been placed without the program. Research also shows that the factors associated with placement of children served are complex and differ by age.

In 1992, Pecora, Fraser, and Haapala (179) wrote that:

[R]esearch findings for the programs within the broad category of family-based services and for the more specific IFPS programs have been contradictory. A variety of family based programs have been evaluated, but many studies have been compromised by poor research designs, limited measures of child or family functioning, inadequate analyses, and small samples.

This lack of demonstrable cause and effect has plagued most, if not all, evaluations of family preservation designs. Throughout the literature, a strong associative link between family preservation intervention and the most often used criterion of effectiveness, preventing a child's removal from his/her birth family, has been elusive. In a meta-analysis of some of the major family preservation programs to date, Rossi (1992, 77) wrote:

Although most of the evaluation of family preservation programs used random-ized experiments or close equivalents and were well carried out, the evaluations reviewed do not provide definitive findings concerning effectiveness.

After going on to say that most designs suffered from small samples, oversimplified analysis, too short a period of time to adequately determine effectiveness, and an "arguably insufficient" effect (avoidance of foster care), Rossi (1992, 97) concludes that the most significant evaluations of family preservation available did not "form a sufficient basis upon which to firmly decide whether family preservation programs are either effective or not."

In an article published in *Child Welfare*, Wells (1994, 481) observed:

Despite broad support for family preservation as a policy, an approach to service delivery, and a program model, sufficient knowledge has accumulated to warrant reconsidering the use of intensive family preservation programs in child welfare practice. Based on an integrative review of the child maltreatment and family preservation literature, the current rationale for programs—the prevention of placement—should be abandoned, and a new rationale should be developed.

In *The Welfare of Children*, respected child welfare investigator Duncan Lindsey (1994, 42) wrote:

> In recent years there have been more than thirty-five evaluations of family preservation in one form or another. The essential requirement of an unbiased test of an experimental study is . . . the use of a randomized control group. . . . [T]hese (randomized control studies) provide the most rigorous and unbiased tests of family preservation and all have found small or insignificant differences as a result of intensive casework services.

Strong additional evidence indicating methodological weaknesses in family preservation service evaluations appeared in a comprehensive review by Heneghan, Horowitz, and Leventhal in *Pediatrics* (1996). The authors' conclusions were quite pessimistic. Somewhat extensive quotations from the article are presented because they speak directly to the issue at hand, that is, measurable outcomes.

> Methodological shortcomings included poorly defined assessment of interventions, inadequate descriptions of the interventions provided, and nonblinded determination of outcomes. Rates of out-of-home placements were 21% to 59% among families who received FPS and 20% to 59% among comparison families. . . . Despite current widespread use of FPS to prevent out-of-home placements of children, evaluations of FPS are methodologically difficult and show no benefit in reducing rates of out-of-home placements of children at risk of abuse and neglect. (535)

> Our review showed that no specified criteria were stated in any study for determining when placement of a child was needed (540). . . . [I]t is unclear whether FPS are "penicillin" or "poison" for families receiving them. . . . Family preservation is not a panacea, yet policy makers have encouraged its widespread adoption. . . . [W]hen children have been abused or neglected, out-of-home placement may be in the child's best interest. As FPS become even more closely incorporated into child protection systems, the net effect may be that placement of children, even when necessary, is discouraged. Applying family preservation to every family, as a matter of policy, may actually be placing children at risk. (541)

The above remarks are hardly benign. That they appeared in *Pediatrics*, a well-respected journal, adds to their credibility. By 1998, additional data questioning the efficacy of continuing family preservation programs were slowly becoming available. We say "slowly" because criticizing family preservation almost automatically places one in the politically incorrect category of violating beliefs that are taken on faith.

In 1988, Congress established the Comprehensive Child Development Program. A family preservation program in all but name, this program contained all the ingredients defining family preservation, such as intensive social work intervention with the most vulnerable and dysfunctional of populations. Traditional family preservation services such as job training, education, parenting classes, counseling, and so forth were offered to the "experimental group" enrolled in the Comprehensive Child Development Program. A "control group" did not receive these services. Comprehensive Child Development Program services were in addition to other types of government subsidies, including food stamps, Medicaid, and others.

After examining the results, an independent evaluation team, Abt Associates, reported that the Comprehensive Child Development Program "did not produce any important positive effects on participating families" (Samuelson 1998, A21). The Comprehensive Child Development Program was abandoned after spending some $325 million. But this program's results were not an aberration in that, like most family preservation designs, they do not work in the aggregate. Nevertheless, despite such negative data, there are powerful forces influencing public policy that keep these programs alive. Of course, this development is not unique. Political currents have long enhanced other local, state, and federal programs that have no empirical support. The "don't-bother-me-with-the-facts" crowd simply ignores the existing data on what serves to better the lives of families and their children, choosing instead to rely on rhetoric.

In a front-page article published by the *New York Times* in April 1997, Peter T. Kilborn reported:

> Overturning the long held premise that keeping families together is the best policy, child welfare officials . . . across the country have been doing everything possible to delay or avoid the return of children to potentially abusive or neglectful families.

Kilborn's article repeats a fundamental tenet of America's child welfare policy: no decision in the name of a child should cause harm to that child. The same article described congressional efforts encouraging the judicial system to "make children's safety, rather than family preservation, their paramount concern."

Federal legislation now makes states eligible for additional federal dollars if they increase the number of adoptions from their foster care systems. Achieving the latter requires the courts to behave in a manner traditionally avoided, namely, making rapid decisions to terminate parental rights. Such actions "would free children for adoption when preserving the family would pose a greater risk to children's safety" (Kilborn 1997).

The literature does report some success using family-based services, in particular intensive family preservation services. In a broad and somewhat sweeping statement, Scannapieco (1993, 509) suggests that "family preservation programs have been found effective in preventing the placement of children outside their homes." But critical to any finding of success, as discussed earlier in this section, is the definition of "effectiveness." Is program success equivalent to the absence of placement or gains in parenting skills? Are population-specific definitions of success pertinent or is success an ubiquitous dynamic?

In an article generally favoring family preservation, Nelson (1997, 111) cites several studies and writes:

> Perhaps the most persuasive evidence of the effectiveness of family preservation programs, however, is the universally high satisfaction both families and workers express with the services.

## Review of Literature Published in 1999

What follows is a review of the literature on family preservation and kinship care articles published in 1999. Contrary to this section's charge to discuss only what is empirically "known" (i.e., data) about these two types of highly touted social interventions, none of the five articles located was an empirical investigation. They have been included nonetheless for two reasons. First, this review demonstrates that family preservation and kinship care continue not to be put to the empirical evaluation test. Second, two of the five appeared as lengthy discussions in highly regarded law reviews (Harvard and Minnesota). That so little scientifically driven data are presented in the literature is telling. Given the fanfare and funding surrounding these programs, it is curious that so little evaluation appears. What the lack of data says to this reviewer is that perhaps we are dealing with what may be the sacred cows of the human service (social work) establishment and its political allies, who are not keen for these approaches to be "put to the (real world) test."

Of the three nonlegal journals in which articles regarding family preservation or kinship care appear, two are well-known social work publications, *Social Work* and *Child Welfare*. The third, the *Journal of Behavioral Health Services and Research*, is less known.

The article appearing in *Social Work* by Denise Burnette describes 74 Hispanic grandparents and great grandparents acting as caregivers (i.e., kinship care) to their grandchildren and great grandchildren. It concludes with what appears to be the obvious: lack of knowledge regarding the types of social programs available was a barrier to utilization of social services.

In *Child Welfare*, Linda Katz presents a nonempirical discussion of concurrent planning. Concurrent planning has developed into an adjunct of family preservation. It's the "ace in the hole" program, simultaneously calling for family preservation efforts aimed either at preventing a child's placement into foster care or reunification from foster care, while developing (hopefully permanent) nonbirth family-based alternatives (i.e., adoption). In speaking of family preservation, Katz suggests:

> Too often, promising new methods have been oversold, inaccurately predict-ing significant cost saving and reduction in placement rates. A useful history lesson results when one considers the fanfare that introduced intensive family preservation services. . . . [These services were] not able to show placement prevention at anything like the rate projected. . . . Evaluators, clinicians, and politicians sought to explain the "lack of success" of family preservation services. It was said the wrong families had been referred, . . . the service not sufficiently standardized, or the wrong outcomes measured. (76)

Given the above statement, the question that comes to mind is: Where are the empirical investigations of "standardized (family preservation) ser-vices" asking the correct questions, with the appropriate families?

In the article appearing in the *Journal of Behavioral Health Services and Research*, M. Staudt spoke with 101 primary caregivers who received family preservation services to determine the extent to which recommended services following family preservation intervention were used. This was not an evaluation of family preservation services per se, but rather an examina-tion of compliance with aftercare suggestions.

In sum, of the three articles broadly examining family preservation and kinship care designs appearing in the above social work focused journals, none were specifically evaluative. All skirted the empirical "so what" ques-tion: Does it matter, demonstrably, if troubled families received family preservation services? Are these families manifestly better off after being recipients of these interventions than they were before? Can the continuance of these programs be justified by data demonstrating, for example, that families receiving family preservation services experience fewer placements of their children into foster care or more reunifications from foster care or greater family stability and functioning as a result of family preservation efforts? In other words, are the results measurable?

In March 1999, the *Harvard Law Review* published an excellent piece entitled, "The Policy of Penalty in Kinship Care." As would be anticipated in a law review article, no empirical data are presented. This four-part presentation succinctly places kinship care in the perspective of the 1996 Personal Responsibility and Work Opportunity Reconciliation Act. Noting what we have already said, that more children than realized when placed into foster care are not placed with strangers (as with traditional foster care) but with relatives in kinship foster care, the piece argues that kin acting as foster parents should be eligible for payments equal to that of nonrelative foster parents.

When the state removes children to kinship settings with payments to the receiving families, it is known as formal kinship care. When there is no state involvement in a child's placement with a family member, it is known as informal kinship care.

The most intriguing of the five articles, by Robert M. Gordon, appeared in the *Minnesota Law Review*, entitled, "Drifting through Byzantium: The Promise and Failure of the Adoption and Safe Families Act of 1997." This legislation (ASFA) was the first to structurally deal with the flaws in PL 96-272, the Adoption Assistance and Child Welfare Act of 1980. ASFA called for (1) reducing foster care drift, (2) a greater emphasis on adoption from the ranks of children already in foster care, and (3) a turning away from asking states to make "reasonable efforts" to return children to their birth parents even when these families were dysfunctional to a point of being dangerous. To a large extent, these three policies form the core of family preservation goals.

In this writer's view, as it relates to this monograph, the main issue is the reasonable efforts idea. Two of family preservation's main goals are either preventing a child's removal into foster care or the unification of children already in foster care with their birth family. The level of a birth family's functioning notwithstanding, many family preservation social workers at times see reunification with a birth family as a victory. Social workers believe in the therapeutic value of families. Social work education reflecting our nation's values sees the family as the best arena within which to raise a child. When a child is reunited with his/her birth family and thus salvaged from the foster care system with the real possibility of drift, it is seen as a real victory, symbolically snatching a child from the jaws of likely disaster.

But at times, these are pyrrhic victories. The nation's newspapers have periodically carried horrendous accounts of children being returned to their birth families in the name of reunification only to later be maimed, mutilated, or even killed (McGrory 1996; Besharov 1996a).

## ❏ PERSONAL RESPONSIBILITY AND WORK OPPORTUNITY RECONCILIATION ACT

This limited discussion of PL 104-193, the Personal Responsibility and Work Opportunity Reconciliation Act of 1996 (PRA), is presented because its effects may have implications for society in general and the continuation of family preservation in particular.

Signed into law by President Clinton in August 1996, PRA eliminated two federal programs, including what had been known for more than 60 years as the federal entitlement program, Aid to Families with Dependent Children (AFDC), and the much more recent Job Opportunities and Basic Skills (JOBS) provisions of the Family Support Act of 1988. A block-granted program known as Temporary Assistance to Needy Families (TANF) supplanted these two programs. TANF is now *the* program through which cash assistance and job training are funneled. Passage of TANF resulted in a fundamental alteration—a paradigm shift if you will—in our basic social welfare philosophy. What TANF accomplished was to move both control of and responsibility for poor children and their families from the federal government to the states, and specifically to the counties (or other local jurisdictions) within those states.[1] Although prior to PRA, welfare standards were federally imposed, AFDC was always individualized at the state level. It is ironic that PRA's passage returned the nation to its historical public assistance origins, giving state and local jurisdictions the responsibility of providing for "their own poor." A new mind-set was also mandated in 1996 that required states and counties to change their expectations of recipients and design radically new intervention systems.

Clients, now referred to as customers, are required to leave TANF rolls after 60 months of assistance. But a state may define 20 percent of their TANF recipients as "hardship" cases, and thereby exempt them from the 60-month limit on assistance. Open-ended entitlements are indeed an artifact of the past. Workfare is the currency of social welfare. Almost every aspect of the public social welfare industry must be restructured. Social welfare interventions now emphasize employment, not eligibility. Today social workers must "custom fit" interventions to meet the needs of individual recipients. Case-specific assessment plans are now required. The application of blanket criteria screening individuals in or out no longer exists. All of the above have but one "customer goal": employment.

PRA not only created TANF; it also impacted other social welfare programs. For example, it radically revised eligibility standards for child care, food stamps, and other programs guaranteed by the entitlement social legislation of the New Deal. Far reaching as these changes are, there are three that fundamentally change the welfare system as we have known it. First, there is no longer a "right" or "entitlement" to public assistance. Second, if eligible, there is a finite period of time during which assistance will be provided (60-month lifetime maximum). Third, employment is the sine qua non of TANF. If states do not meet federally established work rates, penalties are imposed. (See Table 5.) The five-year cap on TANF benefits and how employment is to be interpreted is important vis-à-vis family preservation programs, foster care, and adoption.

As seen in Table 5, for single-parent families, rates of work activity start in 1997 at 25 percent. By 2002, they must reach 50 percent. For two-parent families, rates begin in 1997 at 75 percent and are expected to climb to 90 percent two years later.[2]

An example of the manner in which PRA has radically altered public assistance is that under AFDC single-parent families (mothers, for the most part) were exempted from the work requirement if they had health problems, children under three years of age, and/or "family difficulties." These exclusionary categories no longer exist. Liberal allowances for child care under AFDC have also been dramatically reduced. AFDC allowed for states to tap into an almost limitless amount of federal matching dollars for locally determined amounts of child care. TANF is based on fixed block grants to the states based on the previous year's expenditure.

What impact will PRA generally, and TANF, in particular, have on family preservation programs? The question is not whether there will be an impact,

**TABLE 5**. TANF Mandated Work Activity per Year and Type of Family

| Year | 1997 | 1999 | 2002 |
|------|------|------|------|
| Type of family | | % work activity | |
| Single* | 25 | | 50 |
| Two-parent** | 75 | 90 | |

*Work is defined as 20 hours per week, and 30 hours in 2002.

**Work is defined as 35 hours per week.

but the extent of the impact. What happens when the 60-month limit is reached by the 80 percent of TANF recipients who are not placed in the hardship category and who are either unemployed or underemployed single mothers already faced with a reduction in food stamps under PRA? Will they consider placing their children in foster care for lack of resources to adequately care for them? Will they place their children both informally and formally with relatives in what is now termed "kinship foster care"? Will these once marginally stable families develop consequent problems as a result of PRA's mandates leading to their being labeled dysfunctional and thereby eligible for family preservation intervention? How will these families be impacted by the Adoption and Safe Family Act's requirement that termination of parental rights proceedings be started if a child has been in foster care for 15 of the previous 22 months? What role will adoption play as a result of all this? The answers to these questions and more are unknown as of this writing. Looming over all such questions is the specter of economic recession. Any "economic downturn" will hit hardest those least able to absorb any period of unemployment, or those engaged in minimum-wage, basically unskilled jobs (most often filled by TANF recipients and usually single parents with dependent children).

In sum, within the margins set by federal mandates, the degrees of freedom given to individual states under PRA have allowed for a variety of TANF designs to be implemented. These designs will in turn impact families' ability to cope with and reasonably solve their problems of "everyday living," to get their houses in order prior to expiration of the mandated five-year limit. Barring their ability to provide a nurturing environment for their children, given the current 15-month maximum their children can remain in foster care, termination of parental rights proceedings can be instituted.

## ❏ CONCLUSIONS

Peter Rossi, a social scientist who has written extensively on evaluation research, defines evaluation research as

> . . . the systematic application of social research procedures for assessing the conceptualization, design, implementation, and utility of social intervention programs." (Rossi and Freeman 1993, 5)

Rossi defines meta-analysis as

> . . . the systematic collation and analysis of a series of impact assessments of a program or a related group of programs in order to provide a firm and generalizable estimate of net effects. (214)

Upon examining the debate surrounding the efficacy of family preservation strategies and the extent to which those evaluations followed Rossi's above-described standards, one cannot help but be disappointed. In the materials reviewed for this part of the monograph, "scientific research procedures" and the provision of "firm and generalizable estimate of effects" were not the rule. In fact, the overwhelming majority of social science researchers investigating whether family preservation programs "work"— that they achieved in a measurable way goals set forth by the program's designers—suggest that no strong association was found between this type of intervention and measurable results.

Where then do we go from here? This is not a monograph on alternatives to family preservation interventions, and thus, none will be offered. But the original designers of Homebuilders were well intended. They very much wanted family preservation to be a success. Social conditions cried out for a solution to the malignancy of family dysfunction, the scourge of drugs, the feminization of poverty, and the removal of children from birth families to the temporariness of foster care. All interested individuals wished that family preservation efforts would have been successful, and that they would have demonstrated effectiveness in reducing or eliminating the continuation of children entering foster care. All wished that their efforts had been effective in reducing substance abuse, child abuse and neglect, and family violence. Regrettably, by most accounts, family preservation programming did not achieve any of their intended goals in a convincing manner, and certainly not in a broad enough way to support continuing the policy and the millions of dollars spent to implement it. Family preservation cannot be sustained by political and social rhetoric alone. If data are the currency of evaluation, then family preservation is just about broke.

This writer has consistently taken the position that the field of child welfare knows what works when families cannot for whatever reason successfully nurture a child despite all reasonable efforts. Adoption works, empirically; it is not a blanket panacea but a very real solution when a birth family is unrehabilitative, despite social workers' efforts. Time is usually not on the side of young children. In the real world, there are often no second chances if reunification fails. The latter can lead to the child's being permanently harmed or worse. Social workers must be as close to being absolutely convinced that a family does not pose a threat to a returning (or remaining) child, because all reasonable efforts that have been made to improve a family's level of functioning may not make that family secure and safe. A child should not be returned to his/her birth family for a "trial period" in the name of achieving the goal of family preservation. Social workers must decide what to do when reasonable efforts toward family rehabilitation are not enough to ensure a child's safety. Adoption in such cases should be considered. Where kinship care is appropriate and permanent, that may be considered as the plan of choice. Absence of a blood alternative makes adoption suspect to those wedded to the notion that somehow blood augurs better for a child than nonrelative adoption. The data do not support that notion.

## ENDNOTES

**1.** This is to acknowledge the contributions to certain portions of this discussion by Susan Campbell and Becky Ruppert, M.S.W. students in my spring 1995 research class in child welfare, University of Maryland, School of Social Work, Baltimore, Maryland.

**2.** It is interesting to note that this is not the first time the federal government dictated mandatory work requirements. The Jobs Opportunity and Basic Skills (JOBS) training program of the Family Support Act of 1988 sought to strengthen single mothers' ability to find work by providing education and employment training.

# CHAPTER SEVEN

# Kinship Care

This chapter discusses an alternative to foster care known as kinship care. It has become a popular though somewhat questionable (if not controversial) variant of family preservation programming. In fact, to many, kinship care is family preservation.

For the most part, kinship care is what it sounds like: the full-time care of children by relatives or other adults who have a family relationship to a child whose birth parents, for whatever reason, are unable to provide for them (Wilson and Chipungu 1996). I say "for the most part," because not only are there are no equivalent state guidelines defining what constitutes kinship care, but at times counties within the same state also have different definitions (Wilson and Chipungu 1996). This lack of uniformity is one of the very real weaknesses in kinship care. However, kinship care is generally seen as an alternative to (nonfamilial) foster care. The latter's failure, the reasons for which are almost a constant in the national discourse on welfare reform, is one of the reasons for kinship care's popularity.

## ❏ FACTORS CONTRIBUTING TO THE POPULARITY OF KINSHIP CARE

The growth of kinship care has also been spurred by several other important conceptual, legal, and numerical developments. Legally, two events have been joined—a redefinition of government's role in family (and community) with a "return" to focusing on individual responsibility (i.e., family) as witnessed by passage of PL 104-193, the Personal Responsibility and Work Opportunity Reconciliation Act of 1996 (PRA) (discussed in chapter 6). Emphasizing individual responsibility made reliance on the extended family as responsible foster parents more acceptable. In fact, when foster care is being considered, PRA specifically calls for preference to be given to adult family members over nonrelative foster families.

The second development affecting the growth of kinship care relates to the sheer number of children currently in foster care. A 1998 publication estimates that figure to be upwards of 650,000 children, an almost 50 percent increase since 1992. Most sources use the somewhat more conservative figure of 500,000 children (Hunter College 1998, 3; Nadel 1998, 1). Equally traumatic figures follow: an estimated 15,000 to 100,000 of these children have *no* chance of ever returning to their birth families,[1] and almost 20 percent of these children will be placed with between three and five different foster families in the first few years of their "careers." These are points that champions of family preservation programs curiously overlook when promoting the use of kinship care (National Council for Adoption 1998, 2).

Kinship care has gained in popularity since about the mid-1980s. Indeed, Berrick (1998, 97 n. 7), citing Kusserow (1992), reports that by 1990, about 31 percent of all out-of-home placements were not to foster care but to kinship care. But, as with practically all data concerning child welfare, exact or even relatively accurate figures of how many children are in kinship foster care are hard to come by. The Child Welfare League of America (CWLA 1994, 69) estimated that in 1992 about 4.3 million children lived in some type of "informal" kinship care arrangement, of whom about 900,000 lived with their grandparents. The CWLA (1997, 69) reported that in response to a survey, 14 states in 1995 indicated that some 41 percent of all foster homes were "relative foster homes." The extent to which these figures accurately reflect the true number is difficult to assess.

Several court rulings contributed to the growth of kinship care. Of particular note are two judicial decisions, *L.J. v Massinga* [778 F. Supp. 253; D. Md. (1991)], and *Miller v Youakim* [440 U.S. 125; 99 Sup. Ct. 957 (1979)]. *L.V. v Massinga* involved a consent decree establishing the principle that children in kinship care should be provided with specialized services. In a Supreme Court decision, *Miller v Youakim* prohibited discrimination against children in kinship care for funding under Title IV-E (foster care). Kinship care was also given considerable support in PL 96-272, the Adoption Assistance and Child Welfare Act of 1980. The latter required states to utilize the least restrictive (i.e., most family-like) setting appropriate for each child in foster care.

States have increased the use of kinship care for several reasons, including to maintain children's relationships with their families, to comply with federal standards of child care (PL 96-272), and to reduce costs. Another aspect to consider here is that because foster care payments to families are higher than public assistance benefits, family members eligible for public assistance may opt to provide for a related child in lieu of public welfare (U.S. General Accounting Office 1995).

Kinship care seems to be the permanency plan of choice for African American children as well as children of other races. For example, 50 percent of all court-supervised child care placements in the city of Baltimore are kinship care cases (Jensen 1998, K1).

In her article questioning transracial adoption, Hollingsworth (1998) reviews some of the kinship care literature, citing authors who suggest that confusion exists in regard to foster care statistics. For example, Hollingsworth (1998, 110) cites Barth et al. (1994b) as suggesting that between 1984 and 1989 two-thirds of the increase in California's foster care system could possibly be explained by an increase in kinship foster care; and almost 50 percent of the children placed into New York's foster homes in 1990 were in reality placed in kinship foster homes. The point here is that kinship care is much more widespread a plan of choice than it appears. Although it complies with PL 96-272 (1980), which calls for a child to be placed in the most family-like setting, it apparently contradicts PL 105-89 (1998), which calls for termination of parental rights (TPR) proceedings to begin if a child has been in foster care 15 of the previous 22 months without birth family involvement.

## ❏ KINSHIP CARE AS FOSTER CARE OR FAMILY PRESERVATION?

For many, kinship care is not all that it appears. In agency-sponsored kinship care (as compared to the informal taking in of a child), financial support is usually provided through foster care payments if the home meets state licensing standards for foster care. A limitation is that kinship care policy varies considerably by state, county, and levels of service and support. For example, a study comparing criteria used in selecting kinship care homes found significant variation in state procedures. Although for the most part states hold constant standards for kinship and foster care providers (because kinship care is seen as a variant of foster care), some states may have a different set of criteria for kinship caregivers or permit exceptions from foster care standards (Gleeson and Craig 1994). The most often-cited exception to the rule dealt with the important variable of caregiver training. For the most part, when waivers occurred they were in the direction of more lenient standards required of kinship care providers.

Another study disclosed that foster families received significantly more services than kinship care providers. Once again training was an area given less emphasis for kinship care providers. This 1994 study revealed that not only did 91 percent of kinship caregivers receive no training, but they also had less contact with child welfare agencies than foster care providers. The children themselves were reported as having received less mental health intervention compared with children in foster care (Gleeson and Craig 1994).

In spite of the above, kinship care is seen by many African Americans as a form of family preservation, and not foster care, in that the child remains with its blood family, if not its birth parents. The degree of popularity kinship care enjoys is reflected in the city of Baltimore. One 1993 report indicated that 90 percent of all kinship care families in Baltimore were African American (Dubowitz, Feigelman, and Zuravin 1993). The extent to which kinship care is seen as synonymous with family preservation in the African American community was reflected in a 1997 special issue of *Child Welfare*, titled "Perspectives on Serving African American Children, Youths and Families." In an article titled "Family Preservation and Support Services: A Missed Opportunity for Kinship Care," Danzy and Jackson state the following:

> From an African American perspective, the care of a child by family members other than the biological parents is not child placement but rather family preservation. In the formal child welfare system, however, the transfer of the parenting role to a relative, that is, kinship care, is viewed as child placement. . . . For the African American community, the terms family preservation and kinship care are interchangeable. (37)

The above supports a 1994 statement by Black Administrators in Child Welfare, Inc. It reads, "[We] view kinship care as a component of family preservation services as it gives children a chance to remain with their families" (Danzy and Jackson 1997, 32).

Kinship care then serves the African American community particularly well in that its children are more likely to be either formally placed with, or informally taken in, by blood relatives. The latter type of placement is broadly known as "informal kinship care"; historically, the African American extended family has provided support for children whose parents were unable to do so. In their book on kinship foster care, Hegar and Scannapieco ask this question, "Is kinship foster care out-of-home care or family preservation?" (1999, 5). Their answer to this rhetorical question is that kinship foster care is an out-of-home placement when so ordered by a court. Otherwise, it is defined as an in-home placement. But, they properly link their response to the question of payment. A child placed in an in-home alternative (kinship care, a.k.a. family preservation) other than their birth family is not eligible for federal allowances, whereas an out-of-home placement does carry the promise of federal reimbursement.

## ❏ DISCUSSION OF PROS AND CONS

Recognizing the realpolitik reimbursement plays, the concern of this writer rests not on the distinction between the definition of in-home versus out-of-home placement. A child's best interest should dictate the placement with permanency the goal of any plan. Does a kinship care placement serve a child's best interest? For example, is it permanent, or is it done in the name of family preservation, which is, for many, a flawed policy? This section will demonstrate that in many instances a kinship foster placement keeps the child in a legal and emotional limbo, neither free for adoption nor in a permanent placement. Again, many kinship care environments serve their children well and permanently. But, there is no legal obligation on the part of the kinship care provider to maintain the child until age of majority. Termination of parental rights, albeit a drastic measure, followed by adoption does indeed provide the permanence the law requires and a child needs.

Although exact numbers of children living in kinship care circumstances are not known, we do know something about the demographics of kinship care providers. They are by and large older nonwhite women (many are grandmothers) with restricted financial means who do not see adoption of the children in their care as a plan (Berrick et al. 1994). Since they generally are less involved with social workers (who can suggest ways to cope with problematic situations), research has suggested that kinship care providers have more difficulty setting behavioral standards for their children and in establishing appropriate and realistic parental visitation boundaries (American Humane Association 1997).

Kinship care is not problem-free. In more than a few cases the dysfunctions in a child's birth family can be traced to the birth parents' families of origin or beyond into the extended family. Should the latter exist, why place a child in an environment that may contain the ingredients for further dysfunction? (McLean and Thomas 1996; Grebel 1996) Additionally, there is evidence to suggest that child welfare agencies may not supervise kinship care placements as closely as foster care placements. A New York City study demonstrated that social workers did not supervise kinship placements as closely as they did foster families (Task Force on Permanency Planning for Foster Children 1990); and that when "supervision" was provided, it was more often done by telephoning the kinship foster parent rather than by the required in-person interview (Zwas 1993). A California study reported similar findings as those described in the New York study (Berrick et al. 1994).

Yet another limitation is the likelihood that children in kinship care will remain there longer than children in foster care because agencies may be less likely to plan for adoption. In Maryland, for example, 80 percent of all children adopted are adopted by their foster parents (Fox 1997). A recent Chicago study involving 41 kinship care social workers revealed that this limited sample was considering adoption as a permanent plan for many of the children in kinship care. The negative was that this planning was not being done with the involvement of relevant family members. Adoption was the social worker's final goal, not necessarily the family's (Gleeson, O'Donnell, and Bonecutter 1997).

Other questions include the amount of autonomy kinship caregivers should have, the extent to which federal and state resources should be made available to kinship care families, and the exact role child welfare agencies should play in child protection. Despite its limitations and questionable long-term success, kinship care seems to be the placement of choice when children are removed from their parents. In 1992, more than 30 percent of all children in the custody of state agencies were living with extended family members (Scannapieco and Hegar 1996). In 1995, over 1 million children were in some type of kinship care arrangement. In fact, not only do most states prefer to place children with extended family members, many times it is the only available plan.

Although longitudinal research on kinship care's success is limited, there are some data that indicate all is not well with this type of placement. Dubowitz et al. (1994a) found that children in kinship care have an increased risk of school, behavioral, and health problems. Other studies suggest that when compared with children in foster care, not only are children in kinship care less likely to return home, but adoption is rarely defined as a permanency plan goal (Gleeson and Craig 1994). For this author, one of kinship care's major flaws is the comparative exclusion of adoption as a permanency plan (when all factors indicate adoption as the option of choice) as compared to other (temporary) options.

On the plus side, a 1990 study by the Task Force on Permanency Planning for Foster Children, Inc., based on an examination of about 100 case records, found that even though there was a general lack of state supervision, most kinship care placements were providing adequate supervision for their children. The report suggested that the dysfunction leading to the child's being placed into a relative's home was in most cases limited to the birth parent(s) and not apparent in the kinship care setting. LeProhn (1994) found that kinship care providers are closely involved in all facets of the lives of the children in their charge.

Thornton (1991) designed a study that contrasted permanency plans for children in foster care with kinship care. The results were not surprising. Most kinship caregivers did not want to adopt the children placed with them, although there was little chance of these children returning to their birth families. Many felt that adoption was a needless plan since the child was already living with his/her family (in kinship care). Most verbally agreed to keep the child as long as necessary.

The perspectives of the social workers in Thornton's study were of equal interest. When describing permanency plans (as required by law), social workers indicated that for children in kinship care the plan was usually "independent living" (almost 90 percent). In other words, the child would remain in kinship care until age of majority. In contrast, permanency plans of children in foster care reflected a more even distribution of goals spread among reunification with birth family, adoption, and independent living. Thornton's findings were corroborated in a study by Berrick et al. (1994), which found that indeed most kinship providers would not consider adoption and were of the opinion that children in their care would remain until the age of majority.

Hollingsworth (1998) maintains that African Americans seem reluctant to formally adopt children in their charge (in kinship care), because they believe that since the children are already in their families, formal adoption is not needed.

Adding to the crowded playing field of possible alternatives to conventional adoption (i.e., termination of parental rights and adoption by nonrelatives), Takas and Hegar (1999, 55) propose that yet another category of adoption be designed, which they call "kinship adoption." Kinship adoption as proposed would be a sort of twilight zone between traditional adoption and kinship care.

[K]inship adoption could . . . allow all the permanence of adoption, without completely extinguishing every aspect of the relationship between the children and both birth parents. Kinship adoption could involve either or both of two key differences from traditional adoption:

1. relinquishment or termination of the parental rights of one but not both parents (as in stepparent adoption), and/or

2. relinquishment or termination of some but not all parental rights of both parents (similar to open adoption with enforceable postadoption visitation). (60)

Conceptually, their proposal is intriguing. Operationally, the devil will be in the details, particularly the "relinquishment or termination of some but not all parental rights of both parents."

## ❏ CONCLUSIONS

The objective of this brief discussion was not to provide a thorough review of the literature on kinship care in all its aspects. Its intent was to highlight some of the questionable features of kinship care as they relate to reducing the likelihood of adoption, where adoption would have been the appropriate plan. PL 105-89 calls for adoption to be the permanency plan if a child has been in foster care for 15 of the past 22 months. Kinship care is defined as a type of foster care in an overwhelming number of states and individual cases. Many also see kinship care as a form of family preservation, and as such, in line with the mandates of PL 96-272, thereby forestalling termination of parental rights as the initial step toward adoption. Granted, many kinship care settings appear stable and many providers are dedicated to caring for their children. I believe that however successful kinship care appears to be to some (clearly not to all), it remains by definition a temporary placement. The child is in a new type of long-term impermanence.

## ENDNOTE

**1.** Regrettably, no exact figures exist. The 15,000 figure was cited by Mona Charen in an op-ed for the *Baltimore Sun* (7 October 1997).

# CHAPTER EIGHT

# Impact on Child Welfare of the Multiethnic Placement and Adoption and Safe Families Acts

This chapter discusses two landmark pieces of legislation that this writer believes will impact family preservation programs, the Multiethnic Placement Act (MEPA) of 1996 and the Adoption and Safe Families Act (ASFA) of 1997. Both should profoundly alter the landscape of child welfare "as we know it." Their enforcement should influence the reliance of child welfare agencies on family preservation programs. In the end, if these bills are allowed to play the role for which they were intended, children will be the winners.

Despite strong data supporting the argument that racial and ethnic differences between parental caregivers and adoptees have almost no detrimental effects on a child's (overall) well-being, MEPA was strongly opposed by individuals and groups who continued to see racial and ethnic matching as the sine qua non in any decision to permanently place a child with an available family. Armed once again with an historic agenda comprised of their customary social and political rhetoric, those opposed to a race-blind process of child placement argued their *ad hominem* plaint: race does indeed matter and racially matching a child with custodial parents almost guarantees a positive racial identity and overall healthy persona, whereas ignoring racial similarities between an adoptable child and custodial parents (almost always) works against a child's developing a secure racial identity and healthy persona.

In light of the above, "following the numbers" offers a demographic perspective on America's adoption scene at the end of the century and provides a compelling reason for MEPA's enactment. Between 1980 and 1992, although single white women between the ages of 20 and 45 almost doubled their birth rate, most chose not to place their infants for adoption, reversing decades of behavior by women in similar positions. For example, between 1982 and 1988, the last date for which figures were available, 3 percent of all white mothers relinquished their infants for adoption as compared to 8 percent from 1973 to 1981 (Lewin 1992). The number of white infants available for adoption therefore has been steadily declining. The dearth of available white infants is all the more serious when one realizes that 67 percent of all families waiting to adopt are white. Most put the number of "waiting families" in the hundreds of thousands, and some in the millions (*FACE Facts* 1995). One could say the scarcity of white adoptable infants is "all the more serious," because it is assumed that most white families waiting to adopt would initially prefer a white child.

Although African Americans represent about 12 percent of the total U.S. population, almost 40 percent of all children in foster care free for adoption are black, with almost 50 percent of them waiting for adoptive parents for at least two years.[1] For an additional 69,000 children in foster care, adoption is the goal of social work intervention. Again, a disproportionate number of these children are African American (*FACE Facts* 1995).

These figures demonstrate a very large number of white families wish to adopt and the population of adoptable white children is declining, compared to a large number of available black children for whom there are apparently insufficient black adoptive families. These numbers would strongly suggest that if "a child's best interest" were truly the operative axiom, race would not be a determinant in placing a child with a permanent family. Regrettably, race has historically governed adoption practice.

## ❏ MULTIETHNIC PLACEMENT ACT

In October 1994, President Clinton signed PL 103-382, the Multiethnic Placement Act (MEPA), into law. Sponsored by Ohio Senator Howard Metzenbaum, the bill's intent was to prohibit states and public and private agencies accepting federal money from using race and/or ethnicity as the sole factor in adoption and foster care placement decisions. In other words, it was intended to prohibit the use of racial matching between a waiting child and an available adoptive or foster family. However, as in the case with so many other pieces of legislation, its initial raison d'être was weakened with the inclusion of a number of stipulations. Particularly egregious from my perspective was the "permissible consideration" addition. It reads:

> An agency . . . may consider the cultural, ethnic, or racial background of the child and the capacity of the prospective foster or adoptive parents to meet the needs of the child of this background as one of a number of factors used to determine the best interests of the child.

With the use of the phrase, "may consider the . . . racial background of the child," MEPA diluted its original intent to hold race "harmless" in determining the extent to which a goodness of fit existed between a child and a potential adoptive or foster family. The above inclusion served to thwart any real attempt to move adoption practice forward to the time when race would not be a consideration in adoption. In its altered state, the legislation freed agencies to continue business as usual, to consider a child's racial background when determining placement. This was just what the bill's original supporters sought to eliminate. Additionally, the permissible stipulation consideration shifted the onus of proof to the adoptive parents who had to demonstrate, "capacity . . . to meet the needs of the child of this background. . . ." The term "this background" alludes to the racial differences between the adoptive parents and child.

Clearly, from my perspective, if MEPA had been enacted as originally designed without any changes (which would weaken the prohibition of using racial matching between a waiting child and an available adoptive family), the likelihood is that an unknown number of black children legally free for adoption would have been adopted by waiting white adopters. This would have saved many from the known detrimental effects of that oxymoron called long-term foster care.

The Clinton administration, for reasons of its own, supported additional changes that weakened PL 103-382's original prohibition against the use of race in adoption. The result was that several original supporters of MEPA urged its defeat, including the author of this monograph.

Then, "a funny thing happened on the way to implementation." On 10 May 1996, the House of Representatives passed a new version of MEPA, which not only strengthened the prohibition against using race as a criterion for adoption (with accompanying noncompliance penalties), but also provided for a $5,000 tax credit for families earning $115,000 per year or less who adopt. If a family adopted a special needs child, there would be a $6,000 tax credit. In this new rendering, race could only be a consideration if two equally qualified families of different races sought to adopt the same child. In that case, the family similar in race with the child would be given preference.

This new version of MEPA was endorsed by the President and signed into law in January 1997 as Section 1808, "Removal of Barriers to Interethnic Adoption" of PL 104-188, the Small Business Job Protection Act of 1996. PL 104-188 repealed the "permissible consideration" Section 553 of the 1994 MEPA ("An agency may consider the cultural, ethnic or racial background of the child and the capacity of the prospective . . . adoptive parents to meet the needs of the child . . ."). In the 1997 version, states cannot:

> (A) deny to any person the opportunity to become an adoptive or foster parent on the basis of race, color or national origin of the person . . . or

> (B) delay or deny the placement of a child for adoption or foster care on the basis of race, color or national origin of the adoptive or foster parent, or child, involved.

Section 554, "Required Recruitment Efforts for Child Welfare Services," remained in a strengthened form. This Section is vital for PL 104-188 to succeed. It states that child welfare services:

> provide for the diligent recruitment of potential foster and adoptive families that reflect the ethnic and racial diversity of children in the State for whom foster and adoptive homes are needed.

## ❏ ADOPTION AND SAFE FAMILIES ACT

In 1980, a much heralded piece of legislation was enacted. Known as Public Law 96-272, the Adoption Assistance and Child Welfare Act stated that "reasonable efforts" must be made to prevent a child's entry into foster care through what it termed family preservation (maintenance) programs. If the child was already in foster care, it called for intensive social work intervention with the family of origin with the goal of reuniting the child with the family. By and large, family preservation programs were to have served families where child abuse or neglect occurred or where children had been identified as representing a danger to themselves or others. Families risked having their children temporarily or permanently placed outside the home (foster care) if their dysfunctional behavior persisted. Given the latter, adoption was to be considered (Barth et al. 1994a, 323). To be sure, the primary focus of most PL 96-272 efforts was on the family.

Although the term "child welfare" was prominent in this bill's title, in fact, the child's welfare was secondary to the rehabilitation of the family. Theory guiding this statute was that it was only through a relatively problem-free family that a child could develop his/her potential and minimize, if not eliminate, the possibility of abuse and neglect, the two most frequently cited reasons for a child's entering foster care.

The "reasonable efforts" stipulation maimed PL 96-272. The lack of a clear definition kept most children either in abusive situations or precipitously returned them to parent(s) who were unable to provide adequate environments for them.

That PL 96-272 failed to achieve its broad goal of reducing the number of children entering foster care, even with intensive social work services, led in part to the Adoption and Safe Families Act of 1997. ASFA's intent was to dilute the "reasonable efforts" wording in PL 96-272 and calls on states to quicken the pace at which children leave foster care for more permanent placements (i.e., adoption). It refocuses social service intervention from returning a child to its family of origin to safeguarding a child's security. ASFA, in a real sense, refocuses intervention strategies back to the child. In a relatively short time period (1980 to 1997), the political and social zeitgeist dictated a full-circle turnaround reestablishing an emphasis on a child's well-being, not as a consequence of his/her family's rehabilitation, but many times independent (or in spite) of it. There was a de jure acknowledgment, if not a professional recognition, that family preservation interventions did not succeed in rehabilitating families to the point of reducing the flow of children into foster care or reunifying children from foster care with their families.

ASFA was a real shift from the expectations of PL 96-272, wherein states were free to define "reasonable efforts." Although they remain responsible to make reasonable efforts to return a child to his/her birth family, states will not have this option if the child has been abandoned, physically or sexually abused, or tortured, or if the parents have assaulted or murdered another of their children (Havemann 1997). Additionally, states are now being mandated to initiate termination of parental rights after a child has been in foster care for 15 of the last 22 months. Termination of parental rights is considered the critical step in hastening the exit of children from foster care into adoption.

ASFA contained yet another option, which, by its inclusion in the bill, recognized that family preservation interventions many times do not work. Known as "concurrent planning," it allows the social worker to pursue two opposing permanency plans. With some families, social workers are called upon to simultaneously plan for both the child's removal from the family of origin and develop strategies to eliminate the need for placement outside the family. How this is to occur is not detailed in the statute, except to say that states should seek technical assistance in this regard.

Aside from mandating a reduction from 18 to 12 months for a permanency plan to be developed, ASFA called for another "radical" change in how states deal with child welfare. It called upon the Department of Health and Human Services (DHHS) to design specific outcome measures to evaluate the extent to which states were achieving success in moving children into permanent placements. DHHS is required to report to Congress on each state's progress in achieving the goals described in the outcome criteria.

Senator John Chafee, the bill's sponsor, said, "This historic bill seeks to shorten the time a child must wait to be adopted, all the while ensuring that wherever a child is placed, his or her safety and health will be the first concern" (*Baltimore Sun,* 14 November 1997). "It's time we recognize that some families simply cannot and should not be kept together" (Seeley 1997).

The Adoption and Safe Families Act of 1997 was passed by the House of Representatives in a vote of 406 to 7, and unanimously by the Senate in a voice vote (Havemann 1997).

The next section describes three recent judicial disputes and their implications for family preservation programs.

## ☐ COURT DECISIONS

In late 1997, the *Washington Post* reported that on December 22, a Circuit Court judge awarded custody of a 2-year-old African American to his 23-year-old birth mother. Almost since birth, the child in question had been living with a white foster mother whose petition for adoption the judge rejected (Vogel 1998). Had this been the case's totality it might have been seen as yet another rejection of the positive effects of transracial adoption in favor of a politically correct decision. But, what made the judge's decision more than simply curious was that in 1992, a court in Washington, D.C., convicted the child's mother of murdering her six-month-old daughter and sentenced her to 5 to 15 years in jail. The sentence was suspended immediately. Instead, the mother was placed on probation for three years and ordered to spend weekends in jail. In 1996, the child's mother was convicted of credit card fraud.

It was argued that the judge had no option under current Maryland law other than to return the child to his birth mother. The law stipulates that if a birth parent maintains contact with a child and contributes to its care, other aspects being positive, reunification cannot be denied. A prior conviction of murdering one's own child is not, under current law, sufficient reason to prevent the return of a child to its birth parent. The judge would need fresh grounds for establishing the parent as unfit in order to deny reunification. In this case, the judge said no such evidence existed. In ordering the child returned to his birth mother and denying the foster mother's application for adoption, even though the child's court-appointed attorney recommended adoption by the foster mother, the judge mentioned that it would be more advantageous for the child to be in a racially similar family (Vogel 1998). There are several lingering unanswered questions as to whether this case was decided on its merits or whether racial differences were influential in determining the court's decision (the petitioning foster parent is white and the child is black). In addition, the continual question posed in relation to family preservation is, how many "second chances" is a parent entitled to before the courts say, "Enough, it's time to make the child the primary focus of our attention."

Two of the many responses to the judge's decision were an editorial published on 19 January in the *Wall Street Journal* titled "Fluffy and Mommy," and an op-ed in the 20 January issue of the *Washington Times* by this writer and Rita J. Simon titled "A Child Forsaken." In the former, the point is made that it is near impossible to adopt a cat or dog if one abused or killed a cat or dog in the past. Yet, the same does not hold for humans. Prior abuse or murder, the editorial says, is not grounds to deny someone custody of a child. In the op-ed, we argue that a child's best interest should dictate judicial findings.

On 9 July 1998, the Maryland Court of Special Appeals upheld the judge's decision to return the boy to his birth mother (Janofsky 1998). In August, Maryland's highest court (the Court of Appeals) agreed to hear an appeal of the Special Appeals decision (Seigel 1998; *New York Times* editorial, 9 September 1998). In its decision, the Court of Appeals returned the case to the trial court where a decision was forthcoming at the time of this writing.

Another case, this time in Illinois, had somewhat similar characteristics to the Maryland case, including termination of parental rights and, in the background, the ideology of family preservation. In Chicago, an African American mother with a long history of drug abuse had her three children removed and placed in foster care; the youngest child was placed with a white couple when he was eight days old. Two of the three children were born drug addicted. After two and a half years in foster care, the youngest child's white foster parents filed for adoption, and the state began termination of parental rights proceedings. But, the child's birth mother, now drug free and a certified nursing assistant, not only fought termination of her parental rights but also asked that her son be returned to her. The state said that the birth mother's "volatile and potentially dangerous anger would be directed at her children." That the foster parents were not only white, but a Chicago alderman and an Illinois Appellate Court judge, added to the drama (Belluck 1998).

In continuing to support the foster parents' adoption petition and to proceed with termination of parental rights, a representative of the Illinois Department of Children and Family Services—apparently in reference to provisions in both the Adoption and Safe Families Act of 1997 calling for termination of parental rights and MEPA making adoption as race blind as possible in cases such as the one being described—said her department was in line "with the direction that child welfare systems across the nation are moving in." She also said, "Children cannot be allowed to linger in foster care while parents are given chance after chance after chance to get their acts together" (Belluck 1998). The spokeswoman was supporting what critics of family preservation programs have been charging: When is enough, enough? How many "do-overs" is a parent entitled to before the state puts the well-being of the child ahead of giving a parent yet another second (or third, or fourth. . .) chance? Despite everything, the case was decided in favor of the birth mother (*New York Times*, 5 November 1998).

A minister, echoing what has been heard repeatedly in cases similar to this one, said the intended adopters wanted to ". . . steal the child, his legacy and identity." He added, "[T]here are enough Irish-Catholic children . . . to adopt," referring to the ethnic background of the foster parents.

Finally, in what may be an historic ruling, in September 1998 a Federal District Court judge for Southern New York held that foster parents who want to adopt children who have been in their care for 12 continuous months since infancy and children whose birth parents' rights have been terminated, have similar constitutional guarantees to due process as birth families when child care workers attempt to remove foster children from their care. The judge opined a "constitutionally protected liberty interest in the stability and integrity" of the foster parent-child relationship (Bernstein 1998). This ruling may hold the potential for influencing cases similar to the one in Maryland described above. Since 1977, when the U.S. Supreme Court refused to rule on the rights of foster parents and children placed in their care, courts have consistently held that foster parents and children were not entitled to rights guaranteed to birth families (Bernstein 1998).

# ❑ CONCLUSIONS

This writer believes that both the Multiethnic Placement Act of 1996 and the Adoption and Safe Families Act of 1997 are statutes which, if utilized as they were intended (a big "if"), will challenge even further than a lack of credible results, the efforts made by family preservation programs. As discussed in a previous section, family preservation programs are designed to provide intensive services to families for a limited period of time in order to accomplish several goals, foremost of which are to provide structure to families that would mitigate conditions requiring placement of a child outside the family or to prepare and/or restore familial supports so as to receive a child returning from an out-of-home placement.

For the first time in recent memory two major statutes exist (MEPA and the Adoption and Safe Families Act), which, when seen as complementary, can have real power to protect the future of vulnerable children. The question now is the one raised in the discussion of what is known about family preservation: At what point do social workers say any given adult family members have received all that family preservation has to offer and all benefits of the doubt, yet remain unable to provide the healthy environment their child(ren) require? There are no valid models that specify when this moment occurs. But the decision to remove the child must be made. Proceedings leading to termination of parental rights must be started.

The MEPA and ASFA statutes support the efforts of social workers should a determination be made to remove a child and begin the process of finding a permanent placement. Under the imposed 15 of the previous 22 months' limitation in foster care set by the ASFA for the termination of parental rights proceedings to begin, accompanied by MEPA's mandate not to allow race to be considered when determining a child's permanency plan, vulnerable children from dysfunctional families, perhaps for the first time, have a chance to avoid a life in foster care.

In closing, I would like to repeat what the representative of the Illinois Department of Children and Family said concerning her department's continuing support for termination of parental rights regarding a foster family's adoption petition: "Children cannot be allowed to linger in foster care while parents are given chance after chance after chance to get their acts together" (Belluck 1998). If we substitute the term "a dysfunctional environment" for "foster care" in this quotation, we have the fundamental principle social workers must follow to protect their clients, the children in their charge.

## ENDNOTE

**1.** It must be borne in mind that accurate foster care and adoption figures do not exist since the U.S. government stopped collecting these data in the mid-1970s. For example, some put the number of children legally free for adoption (parental rights have been terminated) at 27,000 (North American Council on Adoptable Children 1995, 1). Others put the figure at 36,000 (Bales 1993).

# CHAPTER NINE

# Transracial Adoption

## ❏ BACKGROUND

Family preservation efforts, at least in urban areas, for the most part involve working with a predominantly African American population. If family preservation interventions fail in their efforts to develop a safe environment for the children involved and the children are either placed in foster care or unable to leave foster care, a permanency plan must quickly be developed.

As described in chapter 8, two federal statutes now exist, the Multiethnic Placement Act (MEPA) and the Adoption and Safe Families Act (ASFA), which make adoption, and in some cases, transracial adoption (TRA), a more likely permanent plan. In any case, ASFA calls for adoption as a permanency plan when a child has been in foster care for 15 of the previous 22 months. Additionally, ASFA reduces the time interval for a permanency plan to be developed from 18 to 12 months.

Any form of adoption provides loving families for children either removed from their birth environments or for children who are unable to return to their families for reasons family preservation interventions simply cannot alleviate. In fact, it may be unfair to even expect family preservation efforts to solve these frequently intractable problems.

Transracial adoption has been a small if controversial part of the U.S. adoption scene for the past 30 years. It generally involves the adoption of African American children by white families. Although, as with any type of adoption, transracial adoption involves power and social class (the comparatively rich adopting the children of the poor), it has the added dimension of race. Transracial adoption consequently brings with it 250 years of the nation's racial history, a history marked by slavery and institutional racism, among other events. Transracial adoption has therefore become a "hot button" issue. It is controversial to the extent that it has been politicized far out of proportion to its numbers. At most, perhaps 30,000 to 35,000 children are involved, although no accurate figures exist. For those opposed to it, transracial adoption is the ultimate expression of white arrogance—the assumption that African Americans cannot provide for their own children and that whites can do it better.

The following literature review on transracial adoption will be divided into two parts. Excluding the work of Simon and Altstein, the first part examines major studies since the early 1970s, when transracial adoption first received serious attention by social science investigators. It concludes with an examination of works completed in 1999. The second part describes my own work with Rita James Simon on transracial adoption beginning in the early 1970s.

## ❏ LITERATURE REVIEW

The work of Lucille Grow and Deborah Shapiro represents one of the earliest studies of transracial adoption. Published in 1974, the major purpose of *Black Children, White Parents* was to evaluate the success of the adoption by white parents of black children. Grow and Shapiro reported that 77 percent of the children had adjusted successfully, and that this percentage was similar to that reported in other studies. They also compared the scores of transracially adopted children with those of inracially adopted white children on the California Test of Personality and found that the scores of the transracially and inracially adopted children were almost the same.

In 1977, Joyce Ladner published a study based on in-depth interviews with 136 parents in Georgia, Missouri, Washington, D.C., Maryland, Virginia, Connecticut, and Minnesota. Before reporting her findings, she introduced a personal note:

> This research brought with it many self-discoveries. My initial feelings were mixed. I felt some trepidation about studying white people, a new undertaking for me. Intellectual curiosity notwithstanding, I had the gnawing sensation that I shouldn't delve too deeply because the findings might be too controversial. I wondered too if couples I intended to interview would tell me the truth. Would

some lie in order to cover up their mistakes and disappointments with the adoption? How much would they leave unsaid? Would some refuse to be interviewed because of their preconceived notions about my motives? Would they stereotype me as a hostile black sociologist who wanted to "prove" that these adoptions would produce mentally unhealthy children? (xii)

By the end of the study, Ladner was convinced that "there are whites who are capable of rearing emotionally healthy black children." Such parents, Ladner continued, "must be idealistic about the future but also realistic about the society in which they now live" (254).

To deny racial, ethnic, and social class polarization exists, and to deny that their child is going to be considered a "black child," regardless of how light his or her complexion, how sharp their features, or how straight their hair, means that these parents are unable to deal with reality, as negative as they may perceive that reality to be. On the other hand, it is equally important for parents to recognize that no matter how immersed they become in the black experience, they can never become black.

Keeping this in mind, such parents should avoid the pitfalls of trying to practice an all-black lifestyle, for it too is unrealistic in the long run, since their family includes blacks and whites and should, therefore, be part of the larger black and white society (254).

Charles Zastrow's 1977 doctoral dissertation compared the reactions of 41 white couples who had adopted a black child against a matched sample of 41 white couples who had adopted a white child. All families lived in Wisconsin, and the two groups were matched on the age of the adopted child and on the socioeconomic status of the adoptive parent(s). All children in the study were preschoolers. Findings indicated similar outcomes for both groups.

When the parents in Zastrow's study were asked to rate their overall satisfaction with the adoptive experience, 99 percent of the transracially adoptive parents and 100 percent of the inracially adoptive parents checked "extremely satisfying" or "more satisfying than dissatisfying." On another measure of satisfaction—one in which the parents rated their degree of satisfaction with certain aspects of their adoptive experience—out of a possible maximum of 98 points, the mean score for the TRA parents was 92.1, and for the IRA parents, 92.0. Zastrow commented as follows:

One of the most notable findings is that TRA parents reported considerably fewer problems related to the care of the child have arisen than they anticipated prior to the adoption. . . . Many of the TRA couples mentioned that they became "color-blind" shortly after adopting; i.e., they stopped seeing the child as a black, and came to perceive the child as an individual who is a member of their family. (81)

Using a mail questionnaire survey in 1981, William Feigelman and Arnold Silverman (1983) compared the adjustment of 56 black children adopted by white families against 97 white children adopted by white families. The parents were asked to assess their child's overall adjustment and to indicate the frequency with which their child demonstrated emotional and physical problems. Silverman and Feigelman concluded that the child's age—not the transracial adoption—had the most significant impact on development and adjustment. The older the child, the greater the problems. They found no relationship between adjustment and racial identity.

W. M. Womack and W. Fulton's study of transracial adoptees and nonadopted black preschool children, published in 1981, found no significant differences in racial attitudes between the two groups of children.

In 1983, Ruth McRoy and Louis Zurcher reported the findings of their study of 30 black adolescents who had been transracially adopted and 30 black adolescents who had been adopted by black parents. In their concluding chapter, McRoy and Zurcher wrote:

> The transracial and inracial adoptees in the authors' study were physically healthy and exhibited typical adolescent relationships with their parents, siblings, teachers, and peers. Similarly, regardless of the race of their adoptive parents, they reflected positive feelings of self-regard. (138)

Throughout their book, the authors emphasized that the quality of parenting was more important than whether the black child had been inracially or transracially adopted:

> Most certainly, transracial adoptive parents experience some challenges different from inracial adoptive parents, but in this study, all of the parents successfully met the challenges. (138)

In 1988, Joan Shireman and Penny Johnson described the results of their study involving 26 inracial (black) and 26 transracial adoptive families in Chicago. They reported very few differences between the two groups of eight-year-old adoptees. Using the Clark and Clark Doll Test to establish racial identity, 73 percent of the transracial adoptees identified themselves as black, compared to 80 percent of the inracially adopted black children. The authors concluded that 75 percent of the transracial adoptees and 80 percent of the inracial adoptees appeared to be doing quite well. They also commented that the transracial adoptees had developed pride in being black and were comfortable in interaction with both black and white people.

Also in 1988, Richard Barth and Marian Berry reported that transracial placements were no more likely to disrupt than other types of adoptions. The fact that transracial placements were as stable as other more traditional adoptive arrangements was reinforced by data presented in 1988 at a North American Council on Adoptable Children (NACAC) meeting on adoption disruption. There it was reported that the rate of adoption disruptions averaged about 15 percent. Disruptions, they reported, did not appear to be influenced by the adoptees' race or gender or the fact that they were placed as a sibling group.

James Rosenthal et al. published a study in 1991 describing a sample of special needs adoptees. The authors found that transracial adoptees were doing reasonably well given that many came from traumatic backgrounds.

Toward the end of 1992 (November–December), a telephone survey of 1,001 Maryland residents over the age of 18 was conducted by the University of Maryland Survey Research Center. My co-author Rita James Simon and I asked four questions. Tables 6, 7, 8, and 9 (N = 984) present the questions and significant findings. A more detailed discussion is beyond the scope of this monograph.

As seen in Table 6, larger proportions of blacks, Asians, and Hispanics compared to whites felt that when a potential adoptive family is considered, racial similarity between the child and potential adopters is indeed important.

The question reproduced in Table 7 excludes a foster family as an option for a black child, offering placement choices between a group home

**TABLE 6.** Responses to: "Choices sometimes have to be made about children in foster care or in institutions such as group homes. In placing such children for adoption, how important is it that a child be placed with a family of his or her own race?"

|                     | Response by race (%) | | | |
|---------------------|-------|-------|-------|----------|
|                     | White | Black | Asian | Hispanic |
| Very important      | 22    | 32    | 33    | 33       |
| Not at all important| 20    | 17    | 20    | 35       |

**TABLE 7.** Responses to: "If a choice had to be made between placing a black child in an institution such as a group home or having a white family adopt the child, which would you prefer?"

|  | Response by race (%) | | | |
|---|---|---|---|---|
|  | White | Black | Asian | Hispanic |
| Institutions | 5 | 10 | 15 |  |
| White family | 88 | 80 | 68 | 85 |

or transracial adoption. Although white respondents led the others, all racial groups overwhelmingly selected transracial adoption as the placement of choice over a group home.

The question appearing in Table 8 is perhaps the most important item since it frames the issue of transracial adoption in a fundamental and stark manner. The critical factor in this item is that it speaks to the temporariness of inracial foster care versus the permanence of transracial adoption. One's response to this question suggests a "bottom line" position on transracial adoption. Among the black respondents there was only a 6 percent difference between those who felt black children should be placed with a black foster family and those who believed a white adoptive family to be the best placement.

The item in Table 9 speaks to the issue of subsidized adoption, a policy Simon and I have long favored and advocated being used to increase inracial adoption. The results were a bit surprising on two levels. The first is that an equal proportion of blacks and whites favored subsidized inracial adoption over transracial adoption. More blacks than whites might have been expected to favor this policy. What this demonstrates is that whites indeed see the merits of inracial adoption and favor subsidies going to black families to assist in their adoption of black children. Interestingly, Asians

**TABLE 8.** Responses to: "If a choice had to be made between placing a black child in foster care with a black family or having a white family adopt the child, which would you prefer?"

|  | Response by race (%) | | | |
|---|---|---|---|---|
|  | White | Black | Asian | Hispanic |
| Black foster care | 31 | 39 | 24 | 14 |
| White family | 58 | 45 | 36 | 70 |

**TABLE 9.** Responses to: "If a choice had to be made between providing financial assistance to a black family who wanted to adopt a black child but could not afford to, or having a white family adopt the child, which would you prefer?"

| | Response by race (%) | | | |
| --- | --- | --- | --- | --- |
| | White | Black | Asian | Hispanic |
| Black family with financial assistance | 55 | 55 | 35 | 47 |
| White family adopt | 31 | 36 | 44 | 43 |

favored TRA over subsidized inracial adoption. Hispanics were almost equally divided on the issue, slightly favoring subsidized adoption.

What these results suggest runs counter to the positions taken by both the National Association of Black Social Workers (NABSW) and the National Association for the Advancement of Colored People (NAACP). While race as a concept is seen as a "very important" or "somewhat important" consideration in adoption by about one-third of all black respondents (Table 6), when the issue is between (inracial) temporariness inherent in foster care and the cross-racial permanence of transracial adoption for black children, 45 percent of black interviewees saw the benefits of transracial adoption as compared to 39 percent favoring inracial foster care (Table 8).

In a 1992 unpublished report, Karen Vroegh, a researcher in the Shireman and associates project, reached the following conclusions:

> The majority of adopted adolescents, whether TRA or IRA . . . , were doing well. The rate and type of identified problems were similar to those found in the general population. Over ninety percent of the TRA parents thought transracial adoption was a good idea.

Christopher Bagley; Arnold Silverman; and Scarr, Weinberg, and Waldman published studies in 1993. The authors of the three works are longtime observers of TRA.

Bagley compared a group of 27 transracial adoptees with a group of 25 inracially adopted whites. Both sets of adoptees were approximately 19 years old, and, on average, were about two years old when adopted. He concluded his study with the following statement:

> The findings of the present study underscore those from previous American research on transracial adoption. Transracial adoption . . . does appear to

meet the psychosocial and developmental needs of the large majority of the children involved, and can be just as successful as inracial adoption. (289)

Upon examining eight empirical surveys of transracial adoption, Silverman found that practically all adoptees made highly satisfactory adjustments, once again reinforcing what had been previously demonstrated.

In 1994, the Search Institute published an impressive study by Peter Benson, Anu Sharma, and Eugene Roehlkepartain, based on a large sample of 881 adolescent adoptees. Of the adoptees, one-third were defined as transracial, which included all nonwhite children (black, Hispanic, recent Asian immigrants, and Native Americans). The authors reported that the transracial adoptees felt more accepted by people of their color than did adoptees of the other two groups. The transracial adoptees also felt that their parents offered more encouragement in matters relating to race and these adoptees were the least apt to want to be another color. In contrast, more transracial adoptees wished their adoptive parents were of a different race than adoptees of the other two groups. Said another way, while more transracial adoptees were comfortable with who they were (black), more would have wished for other-race parents. Presumably, their wish was for black parents. On measures of racial embarrassment, the authors reported that 70 percent of the black transracial adoptees said they never had feelings of racial embarrassment. Seventy-four percent stated they were proud of their race.

In 1995 and 1996, Harris, Blue, and Griffith, and Alexander Rudolph and Carla Curtis, respectively, published reviews of research studies investigating TRA. Harris, Blue, and Griffith's findings strongly supported most previous findings: transracial adoptees and their families were living quite normal lives, quietly going about their business in manners reflecting the rest of society. Adoptees were neither racially confused, nor did they suffer any of the projected disabilities predicted by those with a political agenda bent on demonstrating that this type of adoption is harmful to the adoptees.

Rudolph and Curtis examined 13 empirical investigations of the psychosocial adjustment of transracial adoptees. These authors concluded that most have adjusted well to their interracial experience.

In late 1997, Mark Courtney published a review article in which he argued that the focus on transracial adoption obscures the greater issue of why nonwhite children are overrepresented in the nation's child welfare system (1997a). This writer agrees with Courtney that issues of poverty, child abuse and neglect, high teenage birth rates, and so forth are critical concerns and must be investigated and solutions found. However, efforts aimed at their resolution should not be carried out at the expense of children already in the child welfare system. If nonwhite (and white) children are simply allowed to remain in a foster care system unable to adequately provide for them while society attempts to solve decades-old social problems, we will be sacrificing parentless children for naught. As Courtney points out, it is true that transracial adoption is not a solution to the crisis in foster care, but no one ever said it was.

Devon Brooks and Richard Barth (1999) describe a 17-year longitudinal study of 224 transracial and inracial adoptees of different race/ethnicities and both genders. The adoptees' average age in 1999 was the mid-twenties. Thirty-nine transracially placed black adoptees were included in this study. The authors reported that being the only adopted child in a family of birth children siblings and being male, especially an inracially adopted white male, were negatively related to adjustment. Racial differences between the adoptees and their parents were not significant determinants of overall adjustment patterns.

## Simon-Altstein Research[1]

In 1971–1972, Rita James Simon contacted 206 families living in five cities in the Midwest and asked whether she could interview them about their decision to adopt a nonwhite child. A total of 204 parents and 366 children were interviewed.

Seven years later, Simon and Altstein sought out these families again and were able to locate 71 percent of them, of which 93 percent agreed to participate in the second survey. These parent-only mail or phone interviews focused on their relations with their adopted child(ren) and birth children; the children's racial identity; and the ties that both the adopted birth children had to their larger family units (e.g., grandparents, aunts and uncles), their schools, and their communities.

In fall 1983 and winter 1984, the families were contacted a third time. Ninety-six families agreed to participate. We returned to the original design and conducted personal interviews in the respondents' homes with both the parents and the adolescent children.

The survey focused on how the family members related to each other, the racial identities of the adopted children, the adopted children's sense of integration with their families, and the parents' and children's expectations concerning the children's future identity. We asked about the bonds that the transracial adoptees were likely to have with the mainly white-oriented world of their parents and siblings, and the ties that they were likely to develop with the community of their racial and ethnic backgrounds, or with some composite world.

The fourth and final phase of the study began in 1991. This phase focused almost exclusively on the adult children. Brief telephone interviews were conducted with their parents, mostly to ask them whether, with the knowledge of over 20 years of hindsight, they would have adopted across racial lines, and whether they would advise families like themselves today to adopt a child of a different race.

Lengthy, in-depth personal interviews were conducted only with the children, who were asked to talk about their experiences. In 1990, we were able to contact and interview 98 children, of whom 55 had been transracially adopted, 30 were birth children, and 13 were white adoptees. The median ages of the three groups follow: transracial adoptees, 22; birth children, 26; and white adoptees, 25.

We asked the children to describe how they felt about being the only African American (or Asian American, etc.) person in their family in terms of how it affected their overall personality, sense of security, and identity. What would they have wanted their parents to have done differently? For example, would they have wanted them to have moved into mixed racial neighborhoods rather than continue to live in the predominantly white neighborhoods in which most of the families resided? Were there other aspects of their family life—for example, the churches they attended; the friends the family had; relations maintained with grandparents, aunts, and uncles; or the groups and organizations with which they were involved— that they would have wanted their parents to have changed? Would they have wanted their parents and siblings to have interacted differently with them?

We asked the adult children about their education, the work they were doing, the amount of money they were earning, and whether they were married and had families. We asked them to describe their close friends and the type of community in which they were living. When did they leave their parents' home, and what were the circumstances under which they left? Did they now perceive themselves as integral members of their families? We asked how much time they currently spent with their parents and siblings and how much of their lives they shared with them. What efforts, if any, had they expended on locating their birth parents? If they did seek out one or both birth parents, what motivated them to do so, and how successful were they in locating them?

*The Adoption Experience.* The most important finding that emerged from our first encounter with the families in 1971–1972 was the absence of a white racial preference or bias on the part of the white birth children and the nonwhite adopted children. Contrary to other findings that had been reported up to that time, children reared in these homes appeared indifferent to the advantages of being white, but aware of and comfortable with the racial identity imposed on them by their outward appearance. By and large, the parents of these children were confident that the atmosphere, relationships, values, and lifestyle to which the children were being exposed would enable successful personal adjustments as adults. Transracial adoption appeared to provide the opportunity for children to develop an awareness of race, a respect for the physical differences imposed by race, and an ease with their own racial characteristics, whatever they may be.

When we returned to these families in 1979, we learned that the "extremely glowing, happy portrait" that we had painted seven years earlier now had a few blemishes. We noted that for every five families in which there were the usual pleasures and joys along with sibling rivalries, school-related problems, and difficulties in communication between parent and child, there was one family whose difficulties were more profound and were believed by the parents to have been directly related to the transracial adoption.

Our third survey encounter occurred in 1983–1984 when most of the children were adolescents. We found that almost all of the families had made some changes in their lives. Most of the time, however, the changes were not made because the parents had decided to adopt a child of a different race, but rather because the adoption added another child to the family.

In this phase, all of the children in the study were asked to complete a "self-esteem scale," which in essence measures the respondent's self-respect. A person is characterized as having high self-esteem if she or he considers herself or himself to be a person of worth, and low self-esteem means that the individual lacks self-respect. Because we wanted to make the best possible comparison among our respondents, we examined the scores of our African American transracial adoptees separately from those of the other adoptees and from those of the white birth and adopted children. The scores for all four groups were virtually the same. No one group of respondents manifested higher or lower self-esteem than the others.

The absence of difference among our respondents on the self-esteem scale reminded us of the lack of difference we reported for these children in the first study when we asked them to choose dolls of different races. The scores obtained demonstrated that none of the children manifested a white racial preference.

Our 1977 study was the first to report that there were no white racial preferences among the African American adopted children and the white birth children. The responses suggested that the unusual family environment in which these children were being reared might have caused their deviant racial attitudes and resulted in their not sharing with other American children a sense that being white is preferable to being another race. We noted that the children's responses also demonstrated that their deviant racial attitudes did not affect their ability to identify themselves accurately.

Thus, both sets of our responses—those obtained in 1977 and in 1983–1984—consistently portrayed a lack of difference between African American and white children in these multiracial families, when differences have been and continue to be present between African American and white children reared in the usual single-race family environment. We concluded after the 1983–1984 study that something special seems to happen to both African American and white children when they are reared together as siblings in the same family.

In 1983, we had asked the respondents to identify by race their three closest friends. Seventy-three percent of the transracial adoptees reported that their closest friend was white, and 71 and 62 percent, respectively, said their second and third closest friends were white. In 1990, 53 percent of the transracial adoptees said their closest friend was white, and 70 percent said their second and third closest friends were white. Comparison of the two sets of responses—those reported in 1983 and those given in 1990—show that the transracial adoptees had shifted their close friendships from white to nonwhite and a higher percentage of the birth respondents had moved into a white world.

In 1983, we asked the TRAs and the birth children this question: "Looking ahead to a time when you will not be living in your parents' house, do you expect that you will feel close to them (e.g., discuss things that are bothering you or that you consider important)?" We divided the respondents by sex as well as by adopted status and found that there were no real differences by either category.

Location of birth parents was another issue we raised with the adopted children in the third phase of our study and again in 1990–1991. In 1983–1984, 22.5 percent said they had tried to locate their birth parents; an additional 15 percent said they would like to try; and 25 percent said they were not sure but they might try to locate their birth parents sometime in the future. Thirty-seven percent expressed no interest in locating their birth parents. In 1990–1991, 75 percent said they had not tried to locate either of their birth parents. Among those who did make the effort, only one tried to locate a birth father; the others sought out their birth mothers.

The last part of the 1990–1991 interview focused on finding out how the transracial adoptees felt about the practice of placing nonwhite—especially black—children in white homes, what recommendations they might have about adoption practices, and what advice they might have for white parents who are considering transracial adoption. We also asked the respondents to evaluate their own experience with transracial adoption.

We opened the topic by stating, "You have probably heard of the position taken by the National Association of Black Social Workers (NABSW) and several councils of Native Americans strongly opposing transracial adoption. Do you agree or disagree with their position?" All of the respondents were aware of the NABSW position. Eighty percent of the TRAs and 70 percent of the birth children said they disagreed with the NABSW position. Only five percent of the transracial adoptees agreed with the NABSW position; the others were not sure how they felt about the issue. The reasons most often given for why they disagreed were that "racial differences are not crucial," "transracial adoption is the best practical alternative," and "having a loving, secure relationship in a family setting is all important."

In response to the question, "Would you urge social workers and adoption agencies to place nonwhite children in white homes?", 70 percent of the TRAs and 67 percent of the birth children said "yes," without qualifications or stipulations.

We then shifted to a more personal note and asked, "How do you think being African American (Korean, Native American, etc.) and raised by white parents has affected how you perceive yourself today?" One-third of the TRAs thought the adoption had a positive effect on their self-image. One-third thought it had no effect, and one-third did not know what effect the adoption had on their self-image.

Our next question was this: "All things considered, would you have preferred to have been adopted by parents whose racial background was the same as yours?" Seven percent said yes; 67 percent said no; four percent said they were not sure or did not know; and 22 percent did not answer. When asked why they held the position they did, most said, in essence, "My life has worked out very well"; "My parents love me"; and/or "Race is not that important."

When asked what advice they would give to parents who have the opportunity to adopt a young child of "your racial background," and about how she or he should be reared, 91 percent advised that such parents be sensitive to racial issues, and nine percent advised that they reconsider.

The last question we asked the transracial adoptees was how they would describe their own racial backgrounds. Among the African American transracial adoptees, 32 percent answered black, and 68 percent said they were mixed (mostly black-white, a few black-Asians, and some black-Native Americans). Among the other transracial adoptees, 36 percent described themselves as mixed and 7 percent as white. The other 57 percent labeled themselves Native American, Korean, and Hispanic.

This longitudinal study found that transracial adoptees clearly are aware of and comfortable with their racial identities. Additionally, public opinion surveys show that a majority of Americans—both African American and white—support transracial adoption over institutional living or foster care.

## ❏ CONCLUSIONS

Why did I devote an entire section of this short monograph to describing the above study? I did so because transracial adoption works by any measure, except the measure of social and political rhetoric. This monograph is about family preservation programs and this segment in particular examined the extent to which family preservation efforts are effective. In other words, did they produce measurable results that demonstrated they improved the lives of children and their families by either allowing a child to return home or preventing a child from being removed into foster care? Regrettably, the literature for the most part does not support with empirical evidence the continuance of family preservation programs as currently designed. Yet the problem of dysfunctional families remains. They will not disappear. In fact, given the current economic forecast and federal legislation, pressure on economically marginal families will only increase. Children will remain in jeopardy, and child abuse and neglect may increase as a result. Children will be removed from their birth families. Where will they be placed—in a foster care system already overburdened and inadequate? Unfortunately, perhaps foster care will be the destination for many despite its lack of success and legislation prohibiting its use as a permanent plan. The fortunate children may be placed for adoption. The law says adoption is not an option if foster care is the only plan. Adoption is now mandated.

The fact that dysfunctional families are disproportionately nonwhite can be explained by many social, economic, and political factors. That many of the dysfunctional nonwhite families are African American can be explained by similar factors and the unique experience of blacks in America. But, at the risk of sounding melodramatic, the lives of many thousands of children are at stake if they are left in environments where they are vulnerable to emotional and physical abuse and neglect.

Data on transracial adoption was presented because it is empirically successful and should not be dismissed. It must be considered a viable option open for all children should an inracial permanent placement not be available.

## ENDNOTE

1. The reader is referred to Simon et al., *The Case for Transracial Adoption* (1994) for a more in-depth description of our work.

# PART THREE

## *Responses*

# Commentary
*Ruth McRoy*

Dr. Altstein has presented very compelling yet controversial perspectives about the flaws of family preservation and kinship care and the merits of adoption, especially transracial adoption. He advocates for the removal of children from pathological and dysfunctional families and placement in permanent and secure homes with unrelated caregivers through adoption. In this commentary, I will challenge Dr. Altstein's basic assumptions and conclusions about family preservation, kinship care, and adoption.

## ❏ FAMILY PRESERVATION

Dr. Altstein provides examples of tragic cases in which children have been "brutally abused, even killed, because on the basis of a social worker's evaluation, they were either left with their pathologic family in the name of family preservation or returned from foster care, in the name of 'family reunification.'" He concludes from his review of studies on family preservation outcomes that there is no "definitive data suggesting that family preservation works," and denounces family preservation as being sustained by social and political rhetoric.

I agree with Dr. Altstein that policy changes are needed on behalf of children who have been abused and neglected and who are languishing in foster care. In recent years, there has been an increase in reports of abuse and neglect, an increase in children entering care, a decrease in the number of foster parents available, and a disproportionately high number of children of color, especially African American children, entering the system. However, I suggest that we examine the strengths and weaknesses of family preservation programs in the context of issues facing the child welfare system instead of dismissing the utility of these programs in favor of adoption.

We must begin by looking at some of the systemic reasons increasing numbers of children are coming into care. For example, there continue to be fiscal incentives for public agencies to place children in out-of-home care rather than provide family preservation services. Each year funding for foster care has increased but there have not been similar increases in funding for investigations and support services.

Similarly, public agencies pay foster families as much as $10,000 per year per child, yet family preservation services are budgeted at only $3,000 to $5,000 per year per child. Despite the unequal funding for these services, we are finding evidence that, as a result of family preservation programs, many families are still able to avoid having their children placed in out-of-home care. If preservation services were appropriately funded, even greater benefits could be derived.

Child abuse is caused by many factors, including external stressors such as poverty, substance abuse, racism, and social isolation. Most evaluations of family preservation services have used avoidance of placement as the index of success and most have assessed whether interventions are working in the short term. Additional research is needed to evaluate whether the provision of concrete services such as transportation, affordable housing, emergency shelters and assistance, and substance abuse counseling and treatment may make a difference for low-income families. Few studies have evaluated (1) whether family members have gained skills that persist after intervention, (2) what happens when service periods are extended, and (3) what services work best with specific types of families. We need research that compares outcomes for children placed for adoption versus those who remained in their homes while families received family preservation or kinship care.

The majority of children in the nation's child welfare system come from poor families and disproportionately high numbers of these are children of color. Despite legislation such as the Family Preservation and Support Services Act to reduce the number of foster care entrants, the population of children of color in the system continues to increase. It is premature to conclude that family preservation is not working for these families. In fact, Pinderhughes (1991) has reported that these services are often not targeted toward African American families. As Denby and her colleagues (1998, 13) ask, "Are stereotypes of African American families as dysfunctional and multi-problem leading workers to remove these children from their families and to offer family preservation services to families which are deemed more treatable? When services are provided, are they culturally sensitive and culturally competent?" Before advocating for adoption for these African American children in care, we need to conduct research on outcomes for African American families who have been offered family preservation services and to determine factors that influence protective service workers' decision making about referrals for these services.

Preserving families, if at all possible, is important because biological connectedness is a very significant factor to a child's identity, and separations between parent and child can be devastating. Many suffer traumatic losses when removed from their families and left in the foster care system. Some children view themselves as responsible for the removal. Once in out-of-home care, children can experience multiple placements, more separations, and sometimes abuse, and their sense of security and stability can be undermined.

Ideally, efforts should be made to try to keep children within their families of origin. Workers cannot automatically assume that families don't have the capacity for change. Many of the families served by family preservation programs are amazingly resilient and child welfare workers must identify their strengths and empower them to be successful by providing appropriate supports, including financial assistance.

Although there has been a great deal of media attention given to child deaths in families in which family reunification has occurred, the reality is that this is a very rare occurrence. For example, only about one-tenth of one percent of abuse and neglect cases result in a child death and most of these families had never been reported to protective services. As mentioned in chapter 3, out of 40,000 children served in Families First over a ten-year period, only two fatalities occurred.

## ❏ KINSHIP CARE

Acknowledging that many African American children are being cared for by kinship care providers, Altstein comments that the welfare of many children is not being considered since their caregivers are typically "older nonwhite women . . . with restricted financial means who do not see adoption of the children in their care as a plan." He highlights "questionable features of kinship care" and portrays this practice as a new type of "long-term impermanence." According to Altstein, kinship care keeps children in legal and emotional limbo, neither free for adoption nor in a permanent placement. He calls for social workers to find ways to more quickly identify when interventions are not working and then seek to terminate parental rights to rescue children from destructive environments and place them for adoption.

Kinship care is not a new custom—particularly in African American and other minority families, where children have routinely been "taken in" informally by kin when their birth parents were unable to care for them. Formal kinship care allows the child to maintain a sense of biological connectedness with his or her family of origin and prevents the child from having to experience the many moves and losses associated with placement in foster care. Instead of indicting kinship placements as problematic, we need to acknowledge that the child welfare system has failed to provide adequate services to many of these families. Child welfare staff need to provide the same level of support to these families as foster families and acknowledge what a tremendous asset and strength these families are to the African American community and to the child welfare system.

As mentioned in chapter 1, the Adoption and Safe Families Act aims at moving twice as many children out of foster care annually by 2002. The means by which this goal will be realized include allowances for more flexibility in terminating parental rights, the requirement that permanent placement plans must be established after one year in care, and a financial incentive for states of $4,000 per child adopted above the present adoption levels (Carey 1997a, 1997b). While shortening children's stays in foster care and moving them to a permanent home are noble goals, it is less clear that this policy will benefit children already living within their families in kinship foster care. In some states, over 50 percent of the foster care population is placed with relatives and these families may already view their arrangements as permanent. Forcing the issue of adoption as the only means of achieving permanency may not be an appropriate solution for a large portion of the population this policy intends to serve.

## ☐ ADOPTION

Altstein strongly asserts that "adoption works and is the most successful alternative to birth families" for the many children now in the system and those who will enter the system in the future as a result of changes in welfare benefits and potential economic downturns. He hails two new federal initiatives that will make adoptive placements more likely and "will alter the landscape of child welfare as we know it." The Multiethnic Placement Act and the Interethnic Provisions remove the race-matching practice barriers to transracial placements and provide tax credits for families who wish to adopt; and the Adoption and Safe Families Act allows social workers to do concurrent planning and reduces the time to a permanency plan.

Citing the abundance of available African American children in the child welfare system, the dearth of available white infants, and the large supply of white families seeking to adopt, Altstein proposes that transracial adoptions might be of benefit to all. Moreover, he argues that the new federal adoption policies limiting the time for children to remain in the system and expediting the termination of parental rights will lead to more children needing adoptive placement.

To further validate his support of adoption, Dr. Altstein expresses dismay about two very unusual, highly sensationalized and politicized court cases in which judges have ruled against white foster parents seeking to adopt two African American children in their care. In both cases, African American birth mothers were given another chance to raise their children after the court was given evidence that both had rehabilitated and demonstrated their desire to parent, despite prior criminal convictions in one case and drug use in the other. According to Altstein, in these cases, the judicial system failed to adequately protect the rights of white foster parents and the welfare of the African American children who the foster parents were raising.

Altstein recommends placing children quickly into adoption and preferably transracial adoption in the case of African American children, since he believes African American families are not available. This philosophy has some, albeit unwise, historical precedence as children were taken from poor families and placed with more affluent families; from the days of the orphan trains to the present, many still assume that the welfare of children can be enhanced if raised in a more affluent environment. Some still believe that since whites are more likely to be affluent and devoid of the dysfunctional stereotypes of African American families, these white families are preferable for African American children.

It is important to point out that the assumption that African American families are not available for adoption is false. As I noted in chapter 4, African American families adopt at a rate four times that of white families. In fact, the Child Welfare League of America has acknowledged that African American families can be found for infants, preschoolers, and school-age African American children. The recently established National Center on Permanency for African American Children at Howard University represents a consortium of agencies whose sole purpose is to recruit and place African American children. In many states that have established minority specialist agencies, there are waiting lists of African American families for children.

Moreover, even if same-race placements are not available, one cannot assume that white families are seeking to adopt the children currently in the system. These African American children are mostly school-age and older and many are part of sibling groups. Some have physical or emotional problems as a result of experiencing abuse or neglect.

In reality, the majority of transracial placements that have taken place involve infants, not the older children in the system. The legal cases Altstein cites involve white foster parents seeking to adopt African American infants who have been in their care since birth or soon thereafter. As Courtney (1997, 760) suggests, "Although thousands of African American children and other children of color spend long periods of time in out-of-home care, very few of them exhibit the qualities necessary to move them to the top of the preference lists of the relatively small proportion of potential Caucasian adopters who appear willing to adopt children of color. This appears to be particularly true for African American children in out-of-home care."

The focus on transracial adoptions as the answer is misguided. It is not transracial adoption policies that lead disproportionately large numbers of African American children to be removed from their families and placed in foster care, to remain there for longer periods than other children, and to have a lesser chance of adoption through traditional channels. We need to begin to look at the central problems—poverty, substance abuse, and homelessness, compounded by racism, which lead to the disparate admissions to and treatment of African American children and families in the child welfare system. We need to find ways to eliminate the barriers to service delivery for African American families and children, to identify the strengths of African American families and communities, and to learn from model programs that work, including minority specializing agencies, culturally competent family preservation services, and kinship care. Moreover, significant changes are needed to provide more substantial funding of family preservation services. Child welfare workers need to collaborate with substance abuse professionals to find ways to reduce and prevent the causes of abuse and neglect of children. These initiatives will eventually lead to a reduction in the number of children in the nation's child welfare system.

# Response to McRoy
*Howard Altstein*

Although we may have differing views on the effectiveness of family preservation and kinship care programs, Professor McRoy and I do not seem to disagree on the taken-for-granted assumptions of the U.S. child welfare system that any child's permanency plan must (1) do no harm, (2) conform to the "best interest" axiom, (3) be the least restrictive, and (4) promote permanence.

To avoid controversy and the divisiveness of ideological differences as much as possible, the definition of "what works" in a child's best interest should rest on empirical results of well-designed scientific research. The latter ideally should include large (random) samples followed over long periods of time, comparison groups, controlled interventions, defined outcomes, reliable measuring devices, and safeguards against threats to internal validity. Difficult as it is to construct controlled experiments based on people getting on with their lives, and hungry as we are for results, investigators nevertheless must reject conclusions based on weak, flawed methodologies. To accept these findings as valid not only moves us toward Type II errors, but jeopardizes the development of credible social policy and thus practice, which in turn affect the lives of real children and their families in ways that are not in their best interest.

# ❑ RESEARCH ON FAMILY PRESERVATION AND KINSHIP CARE

Professor McRoy has presented an excellent review of what we know about family preservation and kinship care, including admitted design flaws and shortcomings. The latter are what define most evaluative research of family preservation and kinship care as suspect. That she discusses family preservation programs by theoretical underpinnings is indeed a contribution to the literature.

The matrices comparing results ("proportion of families avoiding placement") of family preservation programs by theoretical framework as demonstrated in Tables 2, 3, and 4, represent an excellent meta-analysis. Upon examining these tables, I find my argument advanced—that is, most evaluative research on family preservation is flawed and unable for the most part to furnish robust data supporting the case for its continuation. For example, the sample sizes for studies of 15 family preservation programs using social learning theory described in Table 2 range from 25 to 678, with four programs having sample sizes of less than 100 and five programs showing no sample size. Twelve of the 15 studies indicate the absence of a control group. Table 3 (family system theory-based programs) describes even weaker designs with four of the eight programs based on sample sizes of less than 100, and two programs reporting no sample sizes. Four of the eight programs show no comparison group data, and in one program, there was no difference in out-of-home placements between the groups. Table 4 (ecological theory-based programs) displays the results of three family preservation programs. Sample sizes are 21, 40, and 327, and none show control groups.

Evaluative data are at best suspect when studies are handicapped by small samples (moreover, it is often unclear whether samples were random); short-term time frames; ambiguous definitions; absence of comparison groups; and where control groups exist, a dearth of convincing data demonstrating meaningful differences between the groups. Supporting the argument that family preservation intervention does not produce hypothesized results was an ambitious four-year study (1989–1993) conducted by the state of Illinois and reported in the literature in 1997. The program was titled "Putting Families First," and this was no ordinary family preservation program. It involved two groups of more than 1,500 families. One group received family preservation intervention (995 families), and the other (569 families) did not (Courtney 1997, 63). At the program's conclusion, Epstein (1997, 53) wrote:

When all is said and done, Putting Families First was an unreliable study of an uncertain intervention, involving groups of subjects that may have been unrepresentative of the study's defining social problem and utilizing unreliable measures of outcomes that may not have any clear meaning.

The process of evaluation involves questioning and a sense of legitimate skepticism until data are generated supporting the program in question. Evaluation does not mean the investigator is searching for programmatic weakness. On the contrary, researchers should make no pro or con statements until the results are in and figures calculated. Evaluation methodology is the "show me" activity of practical research, and works in the best interests of the client.

Evaluating kinship care programs puts one in the position of bucking the trend, not unlike drawing attention to the limitations of family preservation. In fact, it is *de rigueur* to see family preservation and kinship care interventions as effective.

While family preservation is intended to prevent out-of-home placement, kinship care is a form of out-of-home placement. As discussed earlier, kinship care is defined by many not only as a form of family preservation, but the prime alternative when a child requires removal from his/her birth parents. The questions are: Does kinship care fulfill the four canons of our nation's child welfare system? and Does the research show its effectiveness as a long-term, stable environment over other options? Dr. McRoy is indeed correct when she says that kinship care in one form or another is "common practice throughout the world" and that research has shown that children of color are overrepresented in these placements as they are in the overall child welfare system. The task of this book is to determine whether kinship care is demonstrably the best choice compared to other alternatives, that is, that it provides the most nurturing environment and the most effective long-term option for a child.

The 1994 LeProhn and Pecora investigation is recognized as being one of the largest and most detailed of its kind. Their findings indicate that children in kinship care experience about half the number of placements as nonrelative-placed foster care children, and that children in kinship care and foster care effectively spent the same amount of time in care. Research also indicates that children in kinship care receive less professional social work supervision compared to children in foster care.

When comparative group research designs are used, kinship placements are usually contrasted with foster care (in many cases kinship care is referred to as "relative foster care"). Investigators typically compare foster and kinship caregiver demographics (age, income, level of education, marital status, etc.), and move on to describe differences in the two groups of children by age and reason for placement, academic achievement and deportment, number of placements, and so on. One of the weaknesses of comparing kinship care with foster care data is that for the most part foster care research suffers from what plagues most social service evaluative research: a lack of longitudinal, randomized experimental designs contrasting those reared in foster care with those raised in nonfoster care families.

The fact that Dr. McRoy states that "kin placements have been found to be typically more stable than foster placements" is to damn kinship care with faint praise.

## ☐ CONCLUSIONS

Throughout its long and troubled history, transracial adoption has never been defined as a placement of first choice. It has always been a "fallback" permanency plan, second to permanent inracial placement, but superior to any type of temporary plan, inracialness notwithstanding. Additionally, those championing this type of interracial adoption have always, to the best of my knowledge, supported the idea of vigorous recruitment of minority adoptive parents by child welfare agencies. The Child Welfare League of America's current *Standards for Adoption Service* (1988) urges the consideration of transracial adoption only after all efforts at inracial placement have been exhausted, a policy that I have consistently supported. Under the section, "Factors in Selection of Family: Ethnicity and Race," the *Standards* read:

> Children in need of adoption have a right to be placed into a family that reflects their ethnicity or race. Children should not have their adoption denied or significantly delayed, however, when adoptive parents of other ethnic or racial groups are available (34). . . . In any adoption plan, however, the best interests of the child should be paramount. If aggressive, ongoing recruitment efforts are unsuccessful in finding families of the same ethnicity or culture, other families should be considered. (35)

The development of transracial adoption was not a result of deliberate agency programming, but an accommodation to perceived reality. Social change in the areas of abortion, contraception, single parenthood, and reproduction in general had reduced the number of white children available for adoption, leaving nonwhite children as the largest available source.

Changes also occurred regarding the willingness of white couples to adopt nonwhite children.

Those originally opposed to transracial adoption challenged the two main assumptions upon which it rests: (1) that it is necessary to place black children with white families because there are insufficient black families available to adopt black children; and (2) that the benefits derived by a black child in a permanent transracial setting surpass those received in any other temporary (inracial) placement.

It has been suggested that agencies might attempt to subvert the Multiethnic Placement Act's (MEPA) intentions with the (mis)use of family preservation programs and kinship care and by supporting the reintroduction of orphanages. The misgivings regarding family preservation programs revolve around the idea that once a child has been removed (i.e., placed in foster care) from a dysfunctional family in order for time-limited intensive social services to be provided to the family in hopes of rehabilitation, the child will be returned, only to be removed again should familial pathology reappear. Multiple removals would further impair the child. Additionally, time spent in foster care in these circumstances would be time wasted, in that the child is not considered available for a permanent placement and thus could lose opportunities to be placed with an available family.

Family preservation programs, begun with great fanfare, have not "delivered" as originally expected. But, since the time of their inception, family preservation programs and now kinship care have been considered "politically correct" service interventions not to be tampered with too much.[1]

Kinship care allows a child to be placed with a family member however far removed biologically or geographically from a child's nuclear family. In its "Guidance for Federal Legislation," the Administration on Children, Youth and Families (1997, 5) stated that, "other legislative changes which directly affect adoptive and foster care placements . . . [include] the new requirement in Title IV-E that States shall consider relatives as a placement preference for children in the child welfare system."

The apprehension here is that in order to avoid a transracial placement with its demonstrated benefits of permanency, caseworkers will strenuously, and perhaps inappropriately, search for a (racially similar) family member with whom to place an available child. To a very real degree, a child's best interest might be sacrificed at the altar of a questionable inracial placement, even if that placement is with a family member. It is worrisome to many that a relative may not be, in fact, the most appropriate care provider but would be approved and the child placed so as to avoid a cross-racial adoption with perhaps a much more suitable (white) family.

I do not mean to suggest in any manner that all kinship care placements are not in a child's best interest. Many are indeed appropriate intervention goals. What I caution against and am sensitive to are kinship care placements that are arranged simply to avoid a cross-racial placement. Not only is such a practice damaging to a child's best interest, it violates federal law, that is, the MEPA.

In 2000, after almost 30 years of research demonstrating its very positive effects on children and their adoptive families, transracial adoption continues to be opposed, not because it failed to provide a nurturing and permanent environment for children who might otherwise have been assigned to our foster care system, but rather on ideological grounds. Current arguments supporting transracial adoption are nonsequiturs for a very simple reason: most agencies are no longer willing to support this type of adoption as a permanency plan for children, despite the data and despite the MEPA. Never an option for more than a handful of legally free children, transracial adoption will serve even fewer children in need in defiance of the 1964 Civil Rights Act, 1996 and 1997 federal statutes, state legislation, and the Fourteenth amendment to the Constitution (due process).

## ENDNOTE

**1.** For excellent discussions of the data related to family preservation programs, see Barth, Berrick, and Gilbert, eds., *Child Welfare Research Review*, vol. 1 (New York: Columbia University Press, 1994) and U.S. House, *Child Welfare: States' Progress in Implementing Family Preservation and Support Services* (Washington, D.C.: U.S. General Accounting Office, 1997).

# Response to Altstein

*Ruth McRoy*

I agree with Dr. Altstein on the following basic assumptions: any child's permanency plan must (1) do no harm, (2) conform to the "best interest" axiom, (3) be the least restrictive, and (4) promote permanence. Yet, we differ on our view of how these assumptions are operationalized. Basing his promotion of adoption over family preservation on his assessment of published empirical studies of the outcomes of adoption, kinship care, and family preservation, he concludes that the research evidence suggests that "adoption works" while much of the research on family preservation is plagued by empirical flaws. He finds that many family preservation studies lack comparison and/or control groups, utilize small, nonrandomly selected samples, and offer a dearth of convincing data to support family preservation interventions.

Unfortunately, too many social science researchers set out to determine definitively if a practice such as family preservation "works" or is "good or bad," instead of assessing under what circumstances these practices work, for what children and/or parents, and in what types of community contexts. More qualitative research is needed to examine the "process" of preserving a family, the factors that lead some families to be successful candidates for family preservation and others not, and the barriers to treatment effectiveness. Research findings that families are not helped by family preservation services could mean that families are not being properly referred, assessed, or matched with services needed. Rather than condemn the services if they are found not to be working for some, we need to consider why they work for some and what modifications are needed so that they can be successful for other families and children. Moreover, since much of Altstein's argument for adoption is based on the needs of African American children for permanent homes, additional research is needed to determine under what circumstances African American families are even considered as candidates for family preservation services (Pinderhughes 1991).

Professor Altstein suggests that "the task of this book is to determine whether kinship care is demonstrably the best choice compared to other alternatives, that is, that it provides the most nurturing environment and the most effective long-term option for a child." His view is that I "damn kinship care with faint praise" when I state that kin placements have been found to be typically more stable than foster placements. I disagree on both counts. This book cannot determine whether kinship care is the "best choice"; there is no single "best choice" for all children. These decisions must be made on a case-by-case basis. Again, we must determine the circumstances under which kinship care is a viable option. Since African American children are more likely to be placed in kin settings, the finding that kin placements are often more stable than foster placements is very significant. This is especially noteworthy as African American children in out-of-home care are much more likely to move more often and remain in care longer than other children in the system (Stehno 1990). If kin placements offer more stability for African American children, then such placements offer positive options.

Dr. Altstein states that kinship care allows for a child to be placed with a family member far removed biologically or geographically from a child's nuclear family. That is in essence the same policy as foster care. In fact, in some foster placements, children are often deliberately placed far from family members and are also very likely to experience numerous moves while in placement. Moreover, Barth (1997, 296) found in his study of predicted outcomes at six years after placement in nonkinship care in California that African American children were only 25 percent as likely as white children to be reunified with their families. He noted further that African American children were much less likely to be adopted and more likely to remain in foster care than white children. Kinship care offers a very viable alternative for these children. Since they are less likely to be adopted or reunited with their birth family, kinship care makes it possible for them to have stability within their extended family and to meet the criteria of the least restrictive alternative discussed earlier.

In all fairness, Professor Altstein does not denounce all kinship placements. He is most concerned about cases in which such placements are arranged in order to avoid transracial placements. However, most court cases that have pitted a relative against a transracial foster parent in the fight for permanent custody of a child have resulted from the failure of a worker to initially explore the availability of a kin placement prior to making a transracial foster placement (McRoy 1994).

Acknowledging that transracial adoptions have always been a "fallback" to permanent inracial placement, Professor Altstein suggests that such placements have been an accommodation to the perceived reality of large numbers of nonwhite children available for adoption. Dr. Altstein's review of the literature on outcomes of transracial adoption leads him to conclude that almost 30 years of research have demonstrated the "positive effects on children and their adoptive families." However, he fails to critique the body of research on transracial adoptions as he does the literature on kinship care and family preservation. Others (Grotevant 1988; Curtis and Alexander 1996; Hollingsworth 1997; DeBerry, Scarr, and Weinberg 1996) who have critiqued the research literature on transracial placements have noted major flaws with the research. These flaws include the following: lack of appropriate comparison groups; use of descriptive statistics; rare use of multivariate analysis; lack of acknowledgment of study limitations; and a tendency to make global recommendations about transracial adoption policy from methodologically flawed studies. Many studies lacked external validity; were cross-sectional designs; failed to identify determinants of differential outcomes and/or have low internal validity; failed to note that rival hypotheses often exist; and lack discussion of reliability of measures and coding or internal consistency of scales. The few longitudinal studies that have been conducted generally failed to link data across the different waves of data collection, and most had very high attrition rates. Most of the studies failed to define or poorly defined concepts such as racial identity and used unreliable means of measuring the concept. Despite these very serious methodological limitations, many of these studies have concluded that most transracially adopted persons are well adjusted.

It is important to note a recently published longitudinal study, DeBerry, Scarr, and Weinberg (1996), which did utilize multivariate analysis to examine racially and culturally relevant variables utilizing 88 matched-parent transracial adoption cases. At the time of the longitudinal analysis, the adopted persons ranged in age from 16 to 24 years. Although these adoptees had achieved intellectually and academically, there was evidence of unfulfilled needs of belongingness and a higher than expected rate of maladjust-

ment. DeBerry, Scarr, and Weinberg found that the adjustment and ecological competence of transracial adoptees were influenced by the family's
racial socialization process. Of course, these findings need to be replicated,
but they do offer some empirical explanation for some of the anecdotal
evidence of racial identity issues experienced by transracially adopted
persons (McRoy and Zurcher 1983; McRoy, Grotevant, and Zurcher 1988;
McRoy 1999b). This is not presented as an argument against all transracial
adoptions, but is instead a call to help the children and families who are
experiencing problems in such placements.

Despite his advocacy of transracial adoptions, Altstein somewhat
disparagingly acknowledges that transracial placements are still quite un-
popular and will probably not be significantly utilized as an option by
adoption agencies despite MEPA. I agree that transracial adoptions are not
likely to be used as a solution, but for somewhat different reasons than Dr.
Altstein suggests. Removal of barriers to transracial placements will not offer
permanency for the majority of African American children in the nation's
child welfare system (McRoy 1989). Moreover, Barth (1997, 299) notes that
as a whole African American children, regardless of age, "do not have the
same opportunity as other children—all other things being equal—to be
adopted." In fact, according to Barth (1997, 296), "an African American
infant has nearly the same likelihood of being adopted as a Caucasian three-
to five-year-old." We need to find ways to remove barriers that prevent
families of color from adopting (Gilles and Kroll 1991) and to develop
culturally competent recruitment and placement strategies to address the
needs of African American children in the system.

We also need to begin to look at the underlying problems that lead
disproportionately high numbers of African American children to enter the
system in the first place. We must find ways to address poverty, a predictor
of child neglect; inadequate housing; and parental substance abuse, which
together often lead to children entering the system. Prevention services as
well as family preservation services need to be made available to strengthen
African American families and reduce the number of children entering the
system. Finally, we must address the inequities in the child welfare system
that lead African American children to receive fewer services than white
children and to remain in the system longer. We must support programs that
are working, such as kinship care, to prevent more African American
children from lingering in foster care. In fact, kinship placements are more
likely to meet the needs of many more African American children in the
system than transracial placements (Courtney 1997). Similarly, funding must

be sought for adoption and foster care programs and adoption subsidy programs in communities of color.

It is time to put ideology and politics aside and to look clearly at the nation's child welfare system. Inequities exist, and rather than spend time fighting over the pros and cons of family preservation, kinship care, and adoption, we need to acknowledge that all of these services are needed and serve as viable options for some children. Our efforts are best spent in finding ways to make more of these options work, since the future of hundreds of thousands of children rests with each of us.

# Bibliography

Administration on Children, Youth and Families (ACYF), U.S. Department of Health and Human Services. 1995. Multiethnic Placement Act and its effect on adoption. *Families Adopting Children Everywhere (FACE) Facts* 18:12.

———. *Guidance for federal legislation.* 1997. Washington, D.C.: ACYF (log no. ACYF-IM-CB-97-04).

*Adoption and Safe Families Act of 1997.* P.L. 105-89.

*Adoption Assistance and Child Welfare Act of 1980.* P.L. 96-272, 94 Stat. 500.

Ahsan, N. 1996. Revisiting the issues: The Family Preservation and Support Services Program. *The Future of Children* 6:147–56.

Ainsworth, M.D.S. 1985. Attachments across the lifespan. *Bulletin of the New York Academy of Medicine* 61:792–812.

Alexander Jr., R., and C.M. Curtis. 1996. A review of empirical research involving the transracial adoption of African American children. *Journal of Black Psychology* 22:223–35.

Allen, M. 1985. *Report on CSD high impact services.* Salem, OR: State of Oregon Children's Services Division.

Allen, M.L. 1996. *The implications of the Welfare Act for child protection.* Washington, D.C.: Children's Defense Fund.

Altstein, H., and R.J. Simon. 1998. A child forsaken. *Washington Times,* 20 January.

American Humane Association. 1997. *Kinship Care: Protecting Children and Strengthening Families, Child Protection Leader.* Englewood, CO: American Humane Association.

AuClaire, P., and I.M. Schwartz. 1986. *An evaluation of the effectiveness of intensive home-based services as an alternative to placement for adolescents and their families*. Minneapolis: University of Minnesota, Hubert H. Humphrey Institute of Public Affairs.

Azzi-Lessing, L., and L.J. Olsen. 1996. Substance abuse-affected families in the child welfare system: New challenges, new alliance. *Social Work* 41:15–23.

Bagley, C. 1993. Transracial adoptions in Britain: A follow-up study. *Child Welfare* 72:285–9.

Bales, K. 1993. Adoption: The world baby boom. *International Herald Tribune,* 13–14 February.

*Baltimore Sun.* 1997. Bill to cut adoption delays gets approval of Congress. 14 November.

Bandura, A. 1977. *Social learning theory.* Englewood Cliffs, NJ: Prentice-Hall.

Barth, R.P. 1990. Theories guiding home-based intensive family preservation services. In *Reaching high-risk families: Intensive family preservation in human services,* eds. J.K. Whittaker, J. Kinney, E.M. Tracy, and C. Booth, 89–112. New York: Aldine de Gruyter.

———. 1997. Effects of age and race on the odds of adoption versus remaining in long-term out-of-home care. *Child Welfare* 76:285–309.

Barth, R.P., J.D. Berrick, and N. Gilbert, eds. 1994a. *Child Welfare Research Review.* Vol. 1. New York: Columbia University Press.

Barth, R.P., and M. Berry. 1987. Outcomes of child welfare services under permanency planning. *Social Services Review* 61:71–90.

———. 1988. *Adoption and disruption.* New York: Aldine de Gruyter.

Barth, R.P., M. Berry, R. Yoshikami, R.K. Goodfield, and M.L. Carson. 1988. Predicting adoption disruption. *Journal of the National Association of Social Workers* 33:227–33.

Barth, R.P., M. Courtney, J. Berrick, V. Albert, and B.C. Needle. 1994b. "Kinship care: Rights, responsibilities, services and standards." In *From child abuse to permanency planning: Child welfare services, pathways and placements,* eds. R.P. Barth, M. Courtney, J. Berrick, and V. Albert, 195–219. New York: Aldine de Gruyter. Quoted in L.D. Hollingsworth, Promoting same-race adoption for children of color. *Social Work* 43 (1998):110.

Bath, H.L., and D.A. Haapala. 1993. Intensive family preservation services with abused and neglected children: An examination of group differences. *Child Abuse and Neglect* 17:213–25.

———. 1994. Family preservation services: What does the outcome research really tell us? *Social Service Review* September:386–404.

Behavioral Sciences Institute. 1987. *Summary of King, Pierce, Snohomish, and Spokane County Homebuilders Service, September 1, 1986–August 31, 1987.* Federal Way, WA: Behavioral Sciences Institute.

Belluck, P. 1998. In tug-of-war over a toddler, a cry of politics. *New York Times,* 19 September.

Benedict, M.I., S. Zuravin, and R.Y. Stallings. 1996. Adult functioning of children who lived in kin versus non-relative family foster homes. *Child Welfare* 75:529–49.

Benson, P.L., A.R. Sharma, and E.C. Roehlkepartain. 1994. *Growing up adopted: A portrait of adolescents and their families*. Minneapolis, MN: Search Institute.

Berliner, L. 1993. Is family preservation in the best interest of children? *Journal of Interpersonal Violence* 8:556–57.

Bernstein, N. 1998. Judge extends constitutional rights to foster family relationships. *New York Times,* 18 September.

Berrick, J., R. Barth, and B. Needell. 1994. A comparison of kinship foster homes and foster family homes: Implications for kinship foster care as family preservation. *Children and Youth Services Review* 16:33–63.

Berrick, J.D. 1998. When children cannot remain home: Foster family care and kinship care. *The Future of Children* 8:72–87.

Berry, M. 1991. The assessment of imminence of risk of placement: Lessons from a family preservation program. *Children and Youth Services Review* 13:239–56.

———. 1992. An evaluation of family preservation services: Fitting agency services to family needs. *Social Work* 37:314–21.

———. 1994. *Keeping families together*. New York: Garland.

———. 1997. *The family at risk: Issues and trends in family preservation services*. Columbia, SC: University of South Carolina Press.

Besharov, D.J. 1996a. When home is hell: We are too reluctant to take children from bad parents. *Washington Post,* 1 December.

———. 1996b. The children of crack: A status report. *Public Welfare* 54:32–37.

Billingsley, A., and J.M. Giovannoni. 1972. *Children of the storm: Black children and American child welfare*. New York: Harcourt and Brace Jovanovich.

Boston Aging Concerns Young & Old, Inc. 1994. Raising the next generation: A study of grandparents raising grandchildren in Boston. Paper presented at annual conference of the Child Welfare League of America, Washington, D.C.

Bowlby, J. 1969. *Attachment*. Vol. I of *Attachment and loss*. New York: Basic Books.

———. 1980. *Sadness and Depression*. Vol. III of *Attachment and Loss*. New York: Basic Books.

Boyne, J., L. Denby, J.R. Kettenring, and W. Wheeler. 1982. Log-linear models of factors which affect the adoption of "hard-to-place" children. In *Proceedings of the American Statistical Association*, 520–25. Alexandria, VA: American Statistical Association.

Brace, C.L. 1872. *The dangerous classes of New York and twenty years among them*. New York: Wynkoop and Hallenbeck.

Bremner, R.H., ed. 1971. *Children and youth in America: A documentary history, 1865–1965*. Vol. 2. Cambridge, MA: Harvard University Press.

———, ed. 1972. *Children and youth in America: A documentary history*. Vol. 3. Cambridge, MA: Harvard University Press.

Bribitzer, M.P., and M.J. Verdieck. 1988. Home-based, family-centered intervention: Evaluation of a foster care prevention program. *Child Welfare* 67:255–66.

Brody, G.H., and Z. Stoneman. 1992. Child competence and developmental goals among rural black families: Investigating the links. In *Parental belief systems:*

*The psychological consequences for children*, eds. I.E. Sigel, A.V. McGillicuddy-DeLisi, and J.J. Goodnow, 415–32. Hillsdale, NJ: Lawrence Erlbaum
Associates, Inc.

Brooks, D. 1991. Black/white transracial adoption: An update. *OURS* 24:10–21.

Brooks, D., and Barth, R.P. 1999. Adult transracial and inracial adoptees: Effects of
race, gender, adoptive family structure and placement history on adjustment
patterns. *American Journal of Orthopsychiatry* 69:87–99.

Brown, A.W., and B. Bailey-Etta. 1997. An out-of-home care system in crisis:
Implications for African American children in the child welfare system. *Child
Welfare* 76:65–83.

Bryce, M.E. 1978. Client and worker comparison of agency organizational design
and treatment techniques in an intensive home-based social service program
for families. Ph.D. diss., University of Iowa.

Burnette, D. 1999. Custodial grandparents in Latino families: Patterns of service use
and predictors of unmet needs. *Social Work* 44:22–34.

Burt, M.R., and K.J. Pittman. 1985. *Testing the social safety net*. Washington, D.C.:
Urban Institute Press.

Callister, J., L. Mitchell, and G. Tolley. 1986. Profiling family preservation efforts in
Utah. *Children Today* 15:23–25, 36–37.

Caplan, G. 1964. Principles of preventive psychiatry. New York: Basic Books.

Carey, D. 1997a. House overwhelmingly passes foster care adoption bill. *Congressional Quarterly Weekly Report* 55:1024.

———. 1997b. Foster care adoption bill advances to House floor. *Congressional
Quarterly Weekly Report* 55:963.

Charen, M. A chance to give children a childhood. *Baltimore Sun,* 7 October.

*Child Welfare.* 1997. Perspectives on serving African American children, youths and
families (special issue). 76, no. 1.

Child Welfare League of America. 1988. *Standards for adoption service*. Rev. ed. New
York: Child Welfare League of America.

Child Welfare League of America, North American Commission on Chemical Dependency and Child Welfare. 1992. *Children at the front: A different view of the war
on alcohol and drugs*. Washington, D.C.: Child Welfare League of America.

———. 1994. *Kinship care: A natural bridge*. Washington, D.C.: Child Welfare
League of America.

———. 1997. *Child abuse and neglect: A look at the states, 1997 statistical book*.
Washington, D.C.: Child Welfare League of America.

———. 1998. Family foster care fact sheet. Statistics package [accessed 4 February 1999]. Available from INTERNET: http://www.cwla.org/cwla/fostercr/
familyfcfacts98.html.

Children's Defense Fund. 1995. *A Black community crusade and covenant for
protecting children*. Washington, D.C.: Children's Defense Fund.

———. 1996. *The state of America's children yearbook*. Washington, D.C.: Children's
Defense Fund.

Close, M. 1983. Child welfare and people of color: Denial of equal access. *Social Work* 28:13–20.

Costin, L.B. 1985. The historical context of child welfare. In *A Handbook of Child Welfare*, eds. J. Landt and A. Hartman, 34–60. New York: Free Press.

Courtney, M.E. 1994. Factors associated with the reunification of foster children with their families. *Social Service Review* 68:81–108.

———. 1997a. The politics and realities of transracial adoption. *Child Welfare* 76:749–79.

———. 1997b. Reconsidering family preservation: A review of Putting Families First. *Children and Youth Services Review* 19:61–76.

———. 1998. The costs of child protection in the context of welfare reform. *The Future of Children* 8:88–103.

Crosson-Tower, C., ed. 1998. *Exploring child welfare: A practice perspective*. Boston: Allyn and Bacon.

Curtis, C.M., and R. Alexander. 1996. The Multiethnic Placement Act: Implications for social work practice. *Child and Adolescent Social Work Journal* 13:401–10.

Curtis, P.A., and C. McCoullough. 1991. The impact of alcohol and other drugs on the child welfare system. *Child Welfare* 72:533–53.

Daley, S. 1989. Treating kin like foster parents strains a New York child agency. *New York Times,* 23 October.

Danzy, J., and S.M. Jackson. 1997. Family preservation and support services: A missed opportunity for kinship care. *Child Welfare* 76:31–44.

Day, D. 1979. *The adoption of black children: Counteracting institutional discrimination*. Lexington, MA: Lexington Books.

DeBerry, K.M., S. Scarr, and R. Weinberg. 1996. Family racial socialization and ecological competence: Longitudinal assessments of African-American transracial adoptees. *Child Development* 67:2375–99.

Denby, R.W., and K.A. Alford. 1995. Special populations and family preservation: Strengthening our commitment and meeting needs. Paper presented at the National Association of Social Workers Meeting of the Profession, 12–15 October, Philadelphia, Pennsylvania.

Dore, M.M., J.M. Doris, and P. Wright. 1995. Identifying substance abuse in families: A child welfare challenge. *Child Abuse and Neglect* 19:531–53.

Drake, B., M. Berfield, L.A. D'Gama, J.P. Gallagher, M. Gibbs, S. Henry, and D. Lin. 1995. Implementing the family preservation program: Feedback from focus groups with consumers and providers of services. *Child and Adolescent Social Work Journal* 12:391–410.

Dubowitz, H. 1990. The physical and mental health and educational status of children placed with relatives: Final report. Unpublished manuscript. Baltimore, MD: University of Maryland Medical School.

Dubowitz, H., S. Feigelman, and S. Zuravin. 1993. A profile of kinship care. *Child Welfare* 72:153–69.

Dubowitz, H., S. Feigelman, D. Harrington, R. Starr, S. Zuravin, and R. Sawyer.

1994a. Children in kinship care: How do they fare? *Children and Youth Service Review* 16:85–106.

Dubowitz, H., and R.J. Sawyer. 1994b. School behavior of children in kinship care. *Child Abuse and Neglect* 18:899–911.

Eamon, M.K. 1994. Poverty and placement outcomes of intensive family preservation services. *Child and Adolescent Social Work Journal* 11:349–61.

English, D.J. 1998. The extent and consequences of child maltreatment. *The Future of Children* 8:39–53.

Epstein, W.M. 1997. Social science, child welfare, and family preservation: A failure of rationality in public policy. *Children and Youth Services Review* 19:41–60.

Fahlberg, V.I. 1991. *A child's journey through placement*. Indianapolis: Perspectives Press.

*Families Adopting Children Everywhere (FACE) Facts*. 1995. Editor's comment. 18:2, 4.

Fanshel, D., S.J. Finch, and J.F. Grundy. 1989. Foster children in life-course perspective: The Casey Family Program experience [Abstract]. *Child Welfare* 68:467–78.

Feigelman, W., and A. Silverman. *Chosen child—New patterns of adoptive relationships*. New York: Praeger, 1983.

Feldman, L. 1990. *Evaluating the impact of family preservation services in New Jersey*. Trenton, NJ: New Jersey Division of Youth and Family Services, Bureau of Research, Evaluation, and Quality Assurance.

Finkelhor, D., R.J. Gelles, G.T. Hotaling, and M.A. Straus, eds. 1983. *The dark side of families: Current family violence research*. Beverly Hills, CA: Sage.

Forsythe, P.W. 1989. Family preservation in foster care: Fit or fiction? In *Specialist foster family care: A normalizing experience*, eds. J. Hudson, B. Galaway, 63–73. New York: Haworth Press.

———. 1992. Homebuilders and family preservation. *Children and Youth Services Review* 14:37–47.

Fox, L. (Maryland Department of Human Resources). 1997. Interview by Diane Rehm. National Pubic Radio, 10 December.

Fraser, M., and D. Haapala. 1987. Home-based family treatment: A quantitative-qualitative assessment. *Journal of Applied Social Sciences* 12:1–23.

Fraser, M.W., K.E. Nelson, and J.C. Rivard. 1997. Effectiveness of family preservation services. *Social Work Research* 21:138–53.

Garfield, S.L., and A.E. Bergin. 1986. *Handbook of psychotherapy and behavior change*. 3rd ed. New York: Wiley.

Garland, A.F., J.L. Landsverk, R.L. Hough, and E. Ellis-MacLeod. 1996. Type of maltreatment as a predictor of mental health service use for children in foster care. *Child Abuse and Neglect* 20:675–88.

Gelles, R.J. 1996a. *The book of David: How preserving families can cost children's lives*. New York: Basic Books.

———. 1996b. Family preservation: A false promise. *National Resource Center on Child Sexual Abuse News* 5:4.

General Accounting Office. 1997. Child welfare: States' progress in implementing family preservation and support services. Letter report [accessed 9 November 1998]. Available from INTERNET: http://www.gao.gov/AindexFY97/abstracts/he97034.htm.

Gibson, C. 1993. Empowerment theory and practice with adolescents of color in the child welfare system. *Families in Society* 24:387–94.

Gilles, T., and J. Kroll. 1991. *Barriers to same race placement*. St. Paul, MN: North American Council on Adoptable Children.

Gleeson, J., and L. Craig. 1994. Kinship care in child welfare: An analysis of states' policies. *Children and Youth Services Review* 16:7–31.

Gleeson, J.P. 1995. Kinship care and public child welfare: Challenges and opportunities for social work education. *Journal of Social Work Education* 31: 182–93.

———. 1996. Kinship care as a child welfare service: The policy debate in an era of welfare reform. *Child Welfare* 75:419–49.

Gleeson, J.P., J. O'Donnell, and F.J. Bonecutter. 1997. Understanding the complexity of practice in kinship foster care. *Child Welfare* 76:801–26.

Golan, N. 1984. Crisis theory. In *Social work treatment: Interlocking theoretical approaches*, ed. F. Turner, 296–340. New York: The Free Press.

Goldstein, J., A. Freud, and A.J. Solnit. 1973. *Beyond the best interests of the child*. New York: The Free Press.

Gordon, R.M. 1999. Drifting through Byzantium: The promise and failure of the Adoption and Safe Families Act of 1997. *Minnesota Law Review* 83:637–701.

Gray, S.S., and L.M. Nybell. 1990. Issues in African American family preservation. *Child Welfare* 69:513–23.

Grebel, T. 1996. Kinship care and non-relative family foster care: A comparison of care giver attributes and attitudes. *Child Welfare* 75:5–18.

Grigsby, R.K. 1993. Theories that guide intensive family preservation services: A second look. In *Advancing family preservation practice*, eds. E.S. Morton and R.K. Grigsby, 16–18. Newbury Park, CA: Sage.

Grotevant, H.D. 1988. Review of *Transracial Adoptees and Their Families*, by H. Altstein and R.J. Simon. *Contemporary Psychology* 33:853–55.

Grow, L.J., and D. Shapiro. 1974. *Black children, white parents: A study of transracial adoption*. New York: Child Welfare League of America.

Groze, V.K., and J.A. Rosenthal. 1996. *Successful adoptive families: A longitudinal study of special needs adoption*. New York: Praeger.

Gurman, A.S., D.P. Kniskern, and W.M. Pinsof. 1986. Research on the process and outcome of marital and family therapy. In *Handbook of psychotherapy and behavior change*, 3rd ed., eds. S.L. Garfield and A.E. Bergin, 565–624. New York: Wiley.

Haapala, D., V.O. Pina, and C. Sudia, eds. 1991. *Empowering families*. Riverdale, IL: National Association for Family-Based Services.

Haapala, D.A., and J.M. Kinney. 1988. Avoiding out-of-home placement of high-risk status offenders through the use of intensive home-based family preservation services. *Criminal Justice and Behavior* 15:334–48.

Hagedorn, J.M. 1995. *Forsaking our children: Bureaucracy and reform in the child welfare system.* Chicago: Lake View Press.

Hampton, R. 1986. Race, ethnicity and child maltreatment: An analysis of cases recognized and reported by hospitals. In *The black family: Essays and studies*, ed. R. Staples, 172–85. Belmont, CA: Wadsworth.

Harris, H.W., H.C. Blue, and E.E.H. Griffith. 1995. Adoptions and the continuing debate on the racial identity of families. In *Racial and ethnic identity: Psychological development and creative expression*, eds. H.W. Harris, H.C. Blue, and E.E.H. Griffith, 95–114. New York: Routledge.

——, eds. 1995. *Racial and ethnic identity: Psychological development and creative expression.* New York: Routledge.

Hartman, A. 1993. Family preservation under attack. *Social Work* 38:509–12.

*Harvard Law Review.* 1999. The policy of penalty in kinship care. 112:1047–64.

Havemann, J. 1997. Congress acts to speed adoptions. *Washington Post*, 14 November.

Hegar, R.L., and M. Scannapieco, eds. 1999. *Kinship foster care: Policy, practice and research.* New York: Oxford University Press.

Heneghan, A.M., S.M. Horowitz, and J.N. Leventhal. 1996. Evaluating intensive family preservation programs: A methodological review. *Pediatrics* 97:535–42.

Henggler, S.W., G.B. Melton, and L.A. Smith. 1992. Family preservation using multisystemic therapy: An effective alternative to incarcerating serious juvenile offenders. *Journal of Consulting and Clinical Psychology* 60:953–61.

Hill, R.B. 1977. *Informal adoption among black families.* Washington, D.C.: National Urban League, Research Department.

——. 1993. *Research on the African-American family.* Westport, CT: Auburn House.

——. 1997. *The strengths of African American families: Twenty-five years later.* Washington, D.C.: R & B Publishers.

Hinckley, E.C. 1984. Homebuilders: The Maine experience. *Children Today* 13: 14–17.

Hinckley, E.C., and W.F. Ellis. 1985. An effective alternative to residential placement: Home-based services. *Journal of Clinical Child Psychology* 14:209–13.

Hodges, V.G. 1991. Providing culturally sensitive intensive family preservation services to ethnic minority families. In *Intensive family preservation services: An institutional sourcebook*, eds. E.M. Tracy, D.A. Haapala, J. Kinney, and P.J. Pecora, 95–116. Cleveland, OH: Mandel School of Applied Social Sciences, Case Western Reserve University.

Hollinger, J.H. 1998. A guide to the Multiethnic Placement Act of 1994 as amended by the Interethnic Adoption Provisions of 1996. Monograph [accessed 28 October 1998]. Available on INTERNET: http://www.acf.dhhs.gov/programs/cb/special/mepaack.htm.

Hollingsworth, L.D. 1997. Effect of transracial/transethnic adoption on children's racial and ethnic identity and self-esteem: A meta-analytic review. *Marriage and Family Review* 25:99–130.

———. 1998. Promoting same-race adoption for children of color. *Social Work* 43:104–16.

Horejsi, C. 1996. *Assessment and case planning in child welfare and foster care services.* Englewood, CO: American Humane Association.

Hudson, B., and B. Galaway, eds. 1989. *Specialist foster family care: A normalizing experience.* New York: Haworth Press.

Hunter College School of Social Work. 1998. *Permanency Planning Today* 3(Summer).

Iglehart, A.P. 1994. Kinship foster care: Placement, services and outcome issues. *Children and Youth Services Review* 16:107–22.

*Indian Child Welfare Act of 1978,* 25 U.S.C.A. §1901 *et seq.* (West 1983).

Ingram, C. 1996. Kinship care: From last resort to first choice. *Child Welfare* 75:550–66.

Ingrassia, M., and J. McCormick. 1994. Why leave children with bad parents? *Newsweek* 25 April, 52–58.

Janofsky, M. 1998. Court allows boy, 2, to be returned to mother convicted of murder. *New York Times,* 7 November.

Jaudes, P.K., E. Ekwo, and J.V. Voorhis. 1995. Association of drug abuse and child abuse. *Child Abuse and Neglect* 19:1065–75.

Jensen, P. 1998. All in the family. *Baltimore Sun,* 5 July.

Katz, L. 1999. Concurrent planning: Benefits and pitfalls. *Child Welfare* 78:71–87.

Kilborn, P.T. 1997. Priority on safety is keeping more children in foster care. *New York Times,* 29 April.

Kinney, J., D. Haapala, C. Booth, and S. Leavitt. 1988. The Homebuilders model. In *Improving practice technology for work with high-risk families,* eds. J.K. Whittaker, J. Kinney, E.M. Tracy, and C. Booth, 37–67. New York: Aldine de Gruyter.

Kinney, J., D. Haapala, and C. Booth. 1991. *Keeping families together: The Homebuilders model.* New York: Aldine de Gruyter.

Kinney, J.M., B. Madsen, T. Fleming, and D. Haapala. 1977. Homebuilders: Keeping families together. *Journal of Consulting and Clinical Psychology* 45:667–73.

Kroll, J. 1998. Adoption and Safe Families Act of 1997 signed into law. *Adoptalk* Winter:1–2, 9–12.

Kusserow, R. 1992. *Using Relatives for foster care.* Washington, D.C.: U.S. Department of Health and Human Services, Office of Inspector General. Quoted in J.D. Berrick, When children cannot remain home: Foster family care and kinship care. *The Future of Children* 8 (1998):97, ft. 7.

Ladner, J. 1977. *Mixed Families.* New York: Archer Press, Doubleday.

Landt, J., and A. Hartman, eds. 1985. *A Handbook of Child Welfare.* New York: Free Press.

Leeds, S. 1984. *Evaluation of Nebraska's Intensive Services Project.* Iowa City, IA: The National Resource Center on Family Based Service, University of Iowa.

LeProhn, N., and P. Pecora. 1994. *Summary of the Casey foster parent study.* Seattle, WA: The Casey Family Program, Research Department.

LeProhn, N.S. 1994. The role of the kinship foster parent: A comparison of the role conceptions of relative and non-relative foster parents. *Children and Youth Services Review* 16:65–84.

Lewin, T. 1992. Fewer children up for adoption, study finds. *New York Times,* 27 February.

Lewis, R.E., and M. Fraser. 1987. Blending informal and formal helping networks in foster care. *Children and Youth Services Review* 9:153–69.

Lindsey, D. 1991. Factors affecting the foster care placement decision: An analysis of national survey data. *American Journal of Orthopsychiatry* 61:272–81.

———. *The welfare of children.* 1994. New York: Oxford University Press.

Link, M.K. 1996. Permanency outcomes in kinship care: A study of children placed in kinship care in Erie County, New York. *Child Welfare* 75:509–28.

Logan, S., ed. 1996. *Black family strengths, self help and positive change.* Boulder, CO: Westview Press.

Logan, S.M., E.M. Freeman, and R. McRoy, eds. 1990. *Social work practice with Black families: A culturally specific perspective.* New York: Longman.

Lyle, C.G., and J. Nelson. 1983. *Home-based vs. traditional child protection services: A study of the home-based services demonstration project in the Ramsey County Community Human Services Department.* St. Paul, MN: Ramsey County Community Human Services.

Maas, H., and R. Engler. 1959. *Children in need of parents.* New York: Columbia University Press.

MacDonald, H. 1994. The ideology of "family preservation." *Public Interest* Spring: 45–60.

Mason, J., and C. Williams. 1985. The adoption of minority children: Issues in developing law and policy. In *Adoption of children with special needs: Issues in law and policy,* eds. E.C. Segal and M. Hardin, 81–93. Washington, D.C.: American Bar Association.

Mayor's Commission for the Foster Care of Children. 1993. *Family assets: Kinship foster care in New York City.* New York: Department of Health and Human Services.

McCroskey, J., and W. Meezan. 1998. Family-centered services: Approaches and effectiveness. *The Future of Children* 8:54–71.

McDaniel, N., L. Merkel-Holguin, and C. Brittain. 1997. Options for permanency: An overview. *Protecting Children* 13:4–9.

McDonald & Associates. 1992. *Evaluation of Connecticut intensive family preservation services.* Sacramento, CA: Walter McDonald & Associates.

McDonald, T., and J. Marks. 1991. A review of risk factors assessed in child protective services [Abstract]. *Social Services Review,* 65:112–32.

McGrory, M. 1996. Adopt a sense of outrage. *Washington Post,* 12 May.

McKenzie, J. 1993. Adoption of children with special needs. *The Future of Children* 3:62–76.

McLean, B., and R. Thomas. 1996. Informal and formal kinship care populations: A study in contrasts. *Child Welfare* 75:489–505.

McRoy, R. 1989. An organizational dilemma: The case of transracial adoptions. *Journal of Applied Behavioral Science* 25:145–60.

———. 1994. Attachment and racial identity issues: Implications for child placement decision making. *Journal of Multicultural Social Work* 3:59–74.

———. 1996. Racial identity issues for black children in foster care. In *Black family strengths, self help and positive change,* ed. S. Logan, 131–43. Boulder, CO: Westview Press.

———. 1999a. *Special needs adoptions: Practice issues.* New York: Garland.

———. 1999b. *Preserving African American culture: Perspectives on transracial placements.* Los Angeles, CA: Institute for Black Parenting.

McRoy, R., and C. Hall. 1995. Transracial adoptions: In whose best interest? In *Multiracial people in the new millennium,* ed. M. Root, 63–78. Newbury Park, CA: Sage.

McRoy, R., and L.A. Zurcher. 1983. *Transracial and inracial adoptees: The adolescent years.* Springfield, IL: Charles C. Thomas.

McRoy, R., H.D. Grotevant, and L.A. Zurcher. 1988. *Emotional disturbance in adopted adolescents: Origins and development.* New York: Praeger.

McRoy, R., Z. Oglesby, and H. Grape. 1997. Achieving same-race adoptive placements for African American children: Culturally sensitive practice approaches. *Child Welfare* 76:85–104.

Mills, C.S., and D. Usher. 1996. A kinship care case management approach. *Child Welfare* 75:600–18.

Minkler, M., K.M. Roe, and R.J. Robertson-Beckley. 1994. Raising grandchildren from crack-cocaine households: Effects on family and friendship ties of African-American women. *American Journal of Orthopsychiatry* 64:20–29.

Minuchin, S. 1974. *Families and family therapy.* Cambridge, MA: Harvard University Press.

Morisey, P.G. 1990. Black children in foster care. In *Social work practice with black families: A culturally specific perspective,* eds. S.M. Logan, E.M. Freeman, and R. McRoy, 133–47. New York: Longman.

Morton, E.S., and R.K. Grigsby, eds. 1993. *Advancing family preservation practice.* Newbury Park, CA: Sage.

Morton, T. 1993. Ideas in action: The issue is race. *Child Welfare Institute Newsletter* 1–2.

*Multiethnic Placement Act of 1994* (MEPA), P.L. 103-382, 42 U.S.C. §5115a.

Nadel, Mark V. 1998. Foster care: Implementation of the Multiethnic Placement Act poses difficult challenges. Washington, D.C.: Government Accounting Office, GAO/T-HEHS-98-241.

National Adoption Information Clearinghouse (NAIC). 1998. Adoption Statistics—A Brief Overview. Statistics package [accessed 9 November 1998]. Available from INTERNET: http://www.calib.com/naic/.

*National Association of Social Workers News.* 1984. Transracial adoption controversy grows. October:3–4.

National Black Child Development Institute. 1989. *Who will care when parents don't? A study of black children in foster care.* Washington, D.C.: National Black Child Development Institute.

National Commission on Foster Family Care. 1991. *A blueprint for fostering infants, children and youth in the 1990s.* Washington, D.C.: Child Welfare League of America.

National Council for Adoption. 1998. *National Adoption Reports* 19, no. 2.

National Research Council. 1993. *Understanding child abuse and neglect.* Panel on Research on Child Abuse and Neglect, Commission on Behavioral and Social Sciences and Education. Washington, D.C.: National Academy Press.

Nelson, K.E. 1997. Family preservation: What is it? *Children and Youth Services Review* 19:101–18.

Nelson, K.E., and M.J. Landsman. 1991. Must family-centered programs be home-based? In *Empowering families*, eds. D. Haapala, V.O. Pina, and C. Sudia, 25–32. Riverdale, IL: National Assoication for Family-Based Services.

Nelson, K.E., M.J. Landsman, and W. Deutelbaum. 1990. Three models of family-centered placement prevention services. *Child Welfare* 69:3–22.

Newberger, E., R. Reed, J.H. Daniel, J. Hyde, and M. Kotelchuck. 1977. Pediatric social illness: Toward an etiologic classification. *Pediatrics* 60:178–85.

Newlin, P.B. 1997. Family preservation: Where have we been? How can we as social workers continue to collaborate? In *Change and Challenge: MCH Social Workers Make the Difference.* [Proceedings of the BiRegional Conference for Public Health Social Workers, 11–14 June 1995.] Columbia, SC: College of Social Work, University of South Carolina.

*New York Times.* 1998. Ex-addict prevails over powerful foster couple. 5 November.

———. 1998. New respect for foster parents (Editorial). 22 September.

North American Council on Adoptable Children. 1991. *Barriers to race placement.* St. Paul, MN: North American Council on Adoptable Children.

———. 1993. *Transracial adoption position statement.* St. Paul, MN: North American Council on Adoptable Children.

———. 1995. *Adoptalk,* Fall.

*Omnibus Budget Reconciliation Act of 1993,* P.L. 103-66, 107 Stat. 31.

O'Toole, R., P. Turbett, and C. Nalpeka. 1983. Theories, professional knowledge, and diagnosis of child abuse. In *The dark side of families: Current family violence research,* eds. D. Finkelhor, R.J. Gelles, G.T. Hotaling, and M.A. Straus, 349–62. Beverly Hills, CA: Sage.

Paschal, J., and L. Schwahn. 1986. Intensive counseling in Florida. *Children Today* 15:12–16.

Pearson, C.L., and P.A. King. 1987. *Intensive family services: Evaluation of foster care in Maryland, a final report.* Baltimore: Maryland Department of Human Resources.

Pecora, P.J., M.W. Fraser, D.A. Haapala, and J.A. Bartlomé. 1987. *Defining family preservation services: Three intensive home-based treatment programs.* Salt Lake City, UT: University of Utah Social Research Institute.

Pecora, P.J., J.M. Kinney, L. Mitchell, and G. Tolley. 1990. Selecting an agency auspice for family preservation services. *Social Service Review* June: 288–307.

Pecora, P.J., M.W. Fraser, and D.A. Haapala. 1992a. Intensive home-based family preservation services: An update from the FIT project. *Child Welfare,* 71:177–88.

Pecora, P.J., J.K. Whittaker, A.N. Maluccio, R.P. Barth, and R.D. Plotnick. 1992b. *The child welfare challenge: Policy, practice, and research.* New York: Aldine de Gruyter.

Pecora, P.J., M.W. Fraser, and K. Nelson. 1995. *Evaluating family based services.* New York: Aldine de Gruyter.

Pelton, L.H. 1989. *For reasons of poverty: A critical analysis of the public child welfare system in the United States.* New York: Praeger.

———. 1997. Child welfare policy and practice: The myth of family preservation. *American Journal of Orthopsychiatry* 67:545–53.

*Personal Responsibility and Work Opportunity Reconciliation Act of 1996,* P.L. 104-193, 110 STAT. 2105.

Pinderhughes, E.E. 1991. The delivery of child welfare services to African American clients. *American Journal of Orthopsychiatry* 61:599–605.

Rodenhiser, R.W., J. Chandy, and K. Ahmed. 1995. Intensive family preservation services: Do they have any impact on family functioning? *Family Preservation Journal* Summer:69–85.

Rodriguez, P., and A. Meyer. 1990. Minority adoptions and agency practices. *Social Work* 35:528–31.

Ronnau, J., and A.L. Sallee. 1993. *Towards a definition of family preservation: Approach, model, or policy?* Las Cruces, NM: Department of Social Work, New Mexico State University.

Ronnau, J.P., and C.R. Marlow. 1993. Family preservation, poverty, and the value of diversity. *Families in Society: The Journal of Contemporary Human Services* 74:538–44.

Root, M., ed. 1995. *Multiracial people in the new millennium.* Newbury Park, CA: Sage.

Rosenthal, J.A. 1993. Outcomes of adoption of children with special needs. *The Future of Children* 3:77–88.

Rosenthal, J.A., and V. Groze. 1992. *Special needs adoption: A study of intact families.* New York: Praeger.

Rosenthal, J.A., V. Groze, H. Curiel, and P.A. Westcott. 1991. Transracial and inracial adoption of special needs children. *Journal of Multicultural Social Work* 1:13–32.

Rossi, P. 1992. Assessing family preservation programs. *Child and Youth Services Review* 14:77–97.

Rossi, P., and H.E. Freeman. 1993. *Evaluation: A systematic approach.* Newbury Park, CA: Sage.

Rudolph Jr., A., and C.M. Curtis. 1996. A review of empirical research involving transracial adoption of African American children. *Journal of Black Psychology* 22:223–35.

Ryan, K. 1995. Foster care in trouble. *America* 173:15–17.

Samantrai, K. 1992. To prevent unnecessary separation of children and families: Public Law 96-272—Policy and practice. *Journal of the National Association of Social Workers* 37:295–302.

Samuelson, R.J. 1998. Investing in our children. *Wall Street Journal*, 18 February.

Savage, J.J. 1998. Family-centered services for children. In *Exploring child welfare: A practice perspective,* ed. C. Crosson-Tower, 195–222. Boston: Allyn and Bacon.

Scannapieco, M. 1993. The importance of family functioning to prevention of placement: A study of family preservation services. *Child and Adolescent Social Work Journal* 10:509–20.

Scannapieco, M., and R. Hegar. 1995. Kinship care: Two case management models. *Child and Adolescent Social Work Journal* 12:147–56.

———. 1996. A nontraditional assessment framework for formal kinship homes. *Child Welfare* 75:567–82.

Scannapieco, M., and S. Jackson. 1996. Kinship care: The African American response to family preservation. *Social Work* 41:190–96.

Scarr, S., R.A. Weinberg, and I.D. Waldman. 1993. IQ correlations in transracial adoptive families. *Intelligence* 17:541–55.

Schene, P.A. 1998. Past, present, and future roles of child protective services. *The Future of Children* 8:23–38.

Schuerman, J.R., T.L. Rzepnicki, and J.H. Littell. 1992a. *Evaluation of the Illinois Family First placement prevention program: Progress report.* Chicago: Chapin Hall Center for Children.

———. 1994. *Putting families first: An experiment in family preservation.* New York: Aldine de Gruyter.

Schuerman, J.R., T.L. Rzepnicki, J.H. Littell, and S. Budde. 1992b. Implementation issues. *Children and Youth Services Review* 14:193–206.

Seeley, K.Q. 1997. Clinton to approve sweeping shift in adoption. *New York Times,* 17 November.

Seigel, A.F. 1998. Appeal set on decision to return son to woman who killed infant daughter. *Baltimore Sun,* 26 August.

Shireman, J., and Johnson, P. 1988. *Growing up adopted.* Chicago: Chicago Child Care Society, 1988.

Showell, W.H. 1985. *1983–1985 biennial report of CSD's intensive family services.* Salem, OR: Oregon Department of Human Resources, Children's Services Division.

Shyne, A.W., and A.G. Schroeder. 1978. *National study of social services to children and their families*. Washington, D.C.: U.S. Children's Bureau.

Sigel, I.E., A.V. McGillicuddy-DeLisi, and J.J. Goodnow, eds. 1992. *Parental belief systems: The psychological consequences for children*. Hillsdale, NJ: Lawrence Erlbaum Associates, Inc.

Silverman, A. 1993. Outcomes of transracial adoption. *The Future of Children* 3:104–18.

Simon, R., and H. Altstein. 1987. *Transracial adoptees and their families*. New York: Praeger.

Simon, R., H. Altstein, and M. Melli. 1994. *The case for transracial adoption*. Washington, D.C.: American University Press.

Simpson, W.G. 1994. Kinship care and member agencies of the Child Welfare League of America [Abstract]. Unpublished manuscript.

Slaught, E.F. 1993. Reexamining risk factors in foster care. *Children and Youth Services Review* 15:143–54.

*Small Business Job Protection Act of 1996*, P.L. 104-188, H.R. 3448.

Smalley, R. 1967. *Theory for social work practice*. New York: Columbia University Press.

Smith, M.K. 1995. Utilization-focused evaluation of a family preservation program. *Families in Society: The Journal of Contemporary Human Services* January:11–19.

Smith, S.L. 1993. *Family preservation services: State legislative initiatives*. Washington, D.C.: National Conference of State Legislatures.

Staples, R., ed. 1986. *The black family: Essays and studies*. Belmont, CA: Wadsworth.

Staudt, M. 1999. Barriers and facilitators to use of services following intensive family preservation services. *Journal of Behavioral Health Services and Research* 26:39–49.

Stehno, S.M. 1990. The elusive continuum of child welfare services: Implications for minority children and youth. *Child Welfare* 69:551–62.

Steinhauer, P.D. 1991. *The least detrimental alternative: A systematic guide to case planning and decision making for children in care*. Toronto: University of Toronto Press.

Stolley, K. 1993. Statistics on adoption in the United States. *The Future of Children* 3:26–43.

Stroul, B.A. 1988. *Home-based services*. Vol. I of *Series on community-based services for children and adolescents who are severely emotionally disturbed*. Washington, D.C.: CASSP Technical Assistance Center, Georgetown University Child Development Center.

Sullivan, A. 1994. On transracial adoption. *Children's Voice* 3:4–6.

Szasz, T. 1974. *The myth of mental illness: Foundation of a theory of personal conduct*. New York: Harper and Row.

Szykula, S., and M. Fleischman. 1985. Reducing out-of-home placements of abused children: Two controlled field studies. *Child Abuse and Neglect* 9:277–83.

Taft, J. 1937. The relation of function to process in social case work. *Journal of Social Work Process* 1:1–18.

Takas, M., and Hegar, R. 1999. The case for kinship adoption. In *Kinship foster care: Policy, practice and research*, eds. R. Hegar and M. Scannapieco, 55. New York: Oxford University Press.

Task Force on Permanency Planning for Foster Children, Inc. 1990. *Kinship foster care: The double-edged dilemma*. Rochester, NY: Task Force on Permanency Planning for Foster Children.

Testa, M.F., K.L. Shook, L.S. Cohen, and M.G. Woods. 1996. Permanency planning options for children in formal kinship care. *Child Welfare* 75:451–70.

*The Economist*. 1994. Black or white. 33.

Thieman, A.A., and P.W. Dail. 1997. Predictors of out-of-home placement in a family preservation program: Are welfare recipients particularly vulnerable? *Policy Studies Journal* 25:124–39.

Thornton, J.L. 1991. Permanency planning for children in kinship foster homes. *Child Welfare* 70:593–601.

Tracy, E.M., D.A. Haapala, J. Kinney, and P.J. Pecora, eds. 1991. *Intensive family preservation services: An institutional sourcebook*. Cleveland, OH: Mandel School of Applied Social Sciences, Case Western Reserve University.

Tracy, E.M., and J.R. McDonell. 1991. Home-based work with families: The environmental context of family intervention. *Journal of Independent Social Work* 5:93–108.

Tracy, E.M. 1994. Maternal substance abuse: Protecting the child, preserving the family. *Social Work* 39:534–40.

Trattner, W.I. 1994. *From poor law to welfare state: A history of social welfare in America*. 5th ed. New York: Free Press.

Turbett, J.P., and R. O'Toole. 1980. Physician's recognition of child abuse. Paper presented at the annual meeting of the American Sociological Association, New York.

Turner, F., ed. 1984. *Social work treatment: Interlocking theoretical approaches*. New York: The Free Press.

Turner Hogan, P., and S.F. Siu. 1988. Minority children and the child welfare system: An historical perspective. *Social Work* 6:493–98.

University of Pennsylvania School of Social Work. 1990. *The Penn approach: An evolving philosophy of education for social work practice*. Philadelphia: University of Pennsylvania School of Social Work.

U.S. Department of Health and Human Services, Children's Bureau. 1998. *Child maltreatment 1996: Reports from the states to the National Child Abuse and Neglect data system*. Washington, D.C.: U.S. Government Printing Office.

U.S. General Accounting Office (GAO). 1995. Child welfare: Complex needs strain capacity to provide services. Washington, D.C.: General Accounting Office, GAO/HEHS-95-208.

U.S. House of Representatives. 1997. Committee on Ways and Means, Subcommittee on Human Resources, report to the chairman. Child welfare: States' progress in implementing family preservation and support services. Washington, D.C.: General Accounting Office, GAO/HEHS-97-34, B-272396.

Vinokur-Kaplan, D., and A.L. Hartman. 1986. A national profile of child welfare workers and supervisors. *Child Welfare* 65:323–35.

Vogel, S. 1998. Md. custody debate: Did law force judge to return child to killer? *Washington Post,* 13 January.

Vroegh, K. 1992. Transracial adoption: How it is 17 years later. Unpublished report. Chicago: Child Care Society.

Wald, M.S., J.M. Carlsmith, and P.H. Leiderman. 1988. *Protecting abused and neglected children.* Stanford, CA: Stanford University Press.

Walker, C.D., P. Zangrillo, and J.M. Smith. 1994. Parental drug abuse and African-American children in foster care. In *Child welfare research review,* vol. 1, eds. R. Barth, J.D. Berrick, and N. Gilbert, 109–22. New York: Columbia University Press.

*Wall Street Journal.* 1998. Fluffy and mommy (Editorial), 19 January.

Warsh, R., B.A. Pine, and A.N. Maluccio. 1995. The meaning of family preservation: Shared mission, diverse methods. *Families in Society: The Journal of Contemporary Human Services* December:625–26.

Weinberg, R.A., S. Scarr, and I.D. Waldman. 1992. The Minnesota Transracial Adoption Study: A follow-up IQ test performance at adolescence. *Intelligence* 16:117–35.

———. 1992. Intensive family preservation services research: Current status and future agenda. *Social Work Research & Abstracts* 25:21–27.

Wells, K. 1994. A reorientation to knowledge development in family preservation services: A proposal. *Child Welfare* 76:475–88.

Wells, K., and D. Biegel, eds. 1991. *Family preservation services: Research and evaluation.* Newbury Park, CA: Sage.

Wells, K., and E. Tracy. 1996. Reorienting intensive family preservation services in relation to public child welfare practice. *Child Welfare* 75:667–92.

Whittaker, J.K., and E.M. Tracy. 1990. Family preservation services and education for social work practice: Stimulus and response. In *Reaching high-risk families: Intensive family preservation in human services,* eds. J.K. Whittaker, J. Kinney, E.M. Tracy, and C. Booth, 1–11. New York: Aldine de Gruyter.

Whittaker, J.K., J. Kinney, E.M. Tracy, and C. Booth, eds. 1990. *Reaching high-risk families: Intensive family preservation in human services.* New York: Aldine de Gruyter.

Wilson, B.D., and S.S. Chipungu. 1996. Introduction (special issue, Kinship Care). *Child Welfare* 75:387–95.

Womack, W.M., and W. Fulton. 1981. Transracial adoption and the black preschool child. *Journal of American Academy of Child Psychiatry* 20:712–24.

Woodworth, R. 1996. You're not alone . . . You're one in a million. *Child Welfare* 75:619–35.

Zastrow, C.H. 1977. *Outcome of black children–white parents transracial adoptions.* San Francisco: R&E Research Associates.

Zumwalt, J.G. 1997. Nineteen—and alone in the world. *Parade Magazine* December:5–8.

Zwas, M.G. 1993. Kinship foster care: A relatively permanent solution. *Fordham Urban Law Journal* 20:343–73.

# Index

abuse and neglect of children: in
1988, 51; African American
children, 52; causes, 15, 116;
Child Abuse Act Amendments of
1984, 7; drug use, homelessness,
and poverty rates, 66–67; early
prevention measures, 5; economic
pressures, 110; family
preservation services, 16, 67;
family rehabilitation, 91; historical
background, 4–10; incidence
growing, 9; investigations, 7;
kinship care, 35; media accounts,
3; "reasonable efforts" clause, 11,
91; removal as solution, 6;
reported, 52; reporting mandated,
7; risk factors, 12
academic achievement, 39
Addams, Jane, 5
adolescents: academic achievement,
39; adoptees, 100, 103–04; mental
health functioning, 39
adoption: adjustment and racial
identity, 100; African American
attitudes, 86; African American
children, 44–48; after reasonable
efforts, 78; agencies, 131n1;

argument summarized, xi-xii;
bonuses for states, 11; children in
kinship care, 84–85; child's racial
background, 89–90; disruptions,
44, 101; effectiveness, 60, 77;
funding, 70–71; historical
demographics, 87–88; informal,
44–45; inracial adoptions, 45–46;
kinship adoption, 86–87;
long-term benefits, 63; as
permanence option, 55; as race
blind, 94; racial matching, 89–90;
special needs, 8, 43–44; tax credit,
89; transracial adoption, 46–48;
white couples, 47–48
Adoption Assistance and Child Welfare
Act (PL96–272): Homebuilders
model, 20; kinship care
supported, 80–81; reasonable
efforts, 11, 66, 73, 78, 90, 91
adoption plans, for foster care
placements, 9
Adoption and Safe Families Act of
1997 (PL 105–89): adoption
targets and bonuses, 11;
described, 43; goals of, 118;
impact, 91–92; kinship foster care,